The Cobweb Orchestra: a Wonderful Obsession
Memories of the first 18 years by members and friends

Compiled and narrated by Ruth Tanner

Happy Music-making.

Ruth Tanner

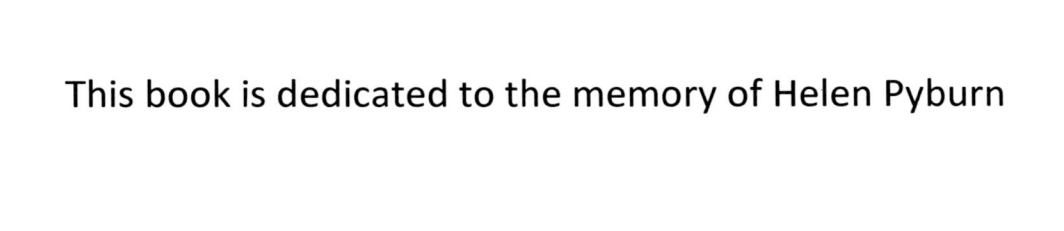

This book is dedicated to the memory of Helen Pyburn

Copyright © Ruth Tanner, 2013

All rights reserved. No part of this book may be reproduced in any form without permission in writing from the author.

ISBN 978-0-9549960-4-8
Published through FoldPress

Contents	Pages
Acknowledgements	1
Foreword	2
1. Right, let's go! How it all Started	4
2. New Groups: The Floodgates Open	15
3. Repertoire: "We're playing WHAT?"	38
4. Makers and Takers: Composers, Arrangers and Others who help to Keep the Show on the Road	46
5. Special Events	61
6. Significant Others: stories of some of those left behind – or not	78
7. Residentials - "A Long Weekend of Music Making with no Distractions"	87
8. Global Connections "Enjoying Sounds"	92
9. Moving Forward	107
10. Spin Offs: From the Intended to the totally Unexpected	114
11. Finding the right instrument	129
12. The Philosophy of Music-making – the Cobweb Way	140
Epilogue	146

Acknowledgements

I have to confess that there have been times over the last few years when I have wondered to myself "Whose idea was this?" Then I remembered that it was mine! It seemed a good idea to try and capture the origin and development of the Cobweb Orchestra over the last eighteen years, some of the highlights, and some of people's most treasured memories.

I have drawn for my material on newsletters, the archive, and most of all on the memories of members of the orchestra and associated friends and well-wishers. It is essentially a compilation of those memories with topics and ideas drawn together by myself as author/editor. I would like to thank everyone who contributed articles for the text, but especially would like to mention a few people whom I have quoted extensively. This is because of the generous amount of text they provided and the richness and humour of the pictures they painted of the Cobweb experience. They are Sheila Blackwell, David Hutton, Tracy Reed, Sheila Ryan and Hilda Sim. Background information from Chris Griffiths and philosophical musings from Stephanie Cant were also invaluable. And of course Andy Jackson was always there to consult on overall approach, and on small details which only he could remember.

My thanks go to all who contributed by writing, by reading the text, advising on production (especially Joan Murray), and helping in a myriad of ways, with a special word of thanks to my husband Brian for support on the IT front, and in every other way possible.

In eighteen years Cobwebs has amassed a considerable history, (as evidenced by the 12 files of archive material) and it has been fascinating, but sometimes tricky, to tease out the details. I have tried to get it right, but any inaccuracies which remain in the telling of this story are entirely mine.

Ruth Tanner
September 2013

Foreword

I have worked with the Cobweb Orchestras every year since 2001, leading them through endlessly rewarding voyages of discovery. Driving all over the North of England, often on stormy winter nights, I have come to value more than I can say these oases of excitement and adventure, kindness and generosity. Having thought of my first Cobweb project as probably a one-off, I have been drawn back again and again by the instinctive love of music radiated by Cobweb musicians, by their fearless sense of adventure in tackling seemingly impossibly difficult music, and by the ever-present sense of joy and excitement that is Cobwebs' hallmark - perhaps owing something to the qualities of Northern communities themselves; of rugged confidence and courage, of an almost childlike love of adventure, and a highly developed sense of fun!

When I was first introduced to Cobwebs I imagined it was another of the concert-focused amateur orchestras which have always been such a strong feature of British musical life, but I quickly began to see quite fundamental differences – more differences than similarities I now think. For Cobwebs, the performance - if one comes at all - is only one part of the journey, and for many people not the most important part. For Cobwebs the entire focus is on the participating musicians, and on their experience and their journey.

That warmly inclusive philosophy which shines radiantly through the pages of this book means players are not judged by regular weekly attendances (which for some would be impractical), but valued each time they appear for the fresh contribution they make to that day's project. This approach also creates a fantastic freedom about repertoire. Cobwebs thrives on giving its musicians an almost literally unbelievable range of repertoire - you only have to look at this year's schedule to see that eclecticism vividly brought to life. I spent a richly enjoyable day helping the musicians get under the mischievous skin of Kurt Weill's 2nd symphony, while other colleagues are leading them through more familiar cornerstones of the repertoire. On another day the Composers and Arrangers and Guinea Pig Orchestras offer a near-unique opportunity for Cobweb musicians to hear their own work played, while another day might see a wild romp through John Williams' rumbustious Star Wars score or the players tackling Stravinsky's legendarily complex Rite of Spring.

Looking back on 10 years of happy, rewarding music-making with these inspirational people, how do I see them? My memories of our work together have always been – above all – that it has been fun. Together we have enjoyed being inquisitive, and for many of the less experienced musicians the sessions have also been deeply courageous experiences – daring to expose their developing experience in ways that would be almost unimaginable in a conventional amateur orchestra.

The Cobweb projects I've experienced have been characterised by a wonderfully impatient disregard of just about all the normal classical conventions, asking only that the musicians' experience brings them (all of them, Cobwebs has the most unselfish working ethic you could imagine) into direct, personal contact with the music. I like to think that many of the composers whose music we have learned together sat at their own desks gripped by just that sense of adventure, of discovery, of joy. Long may Cobwebs flourish, and continue to treat all the received traditions and expectations surrounding classical music with glorious irreverence, asking only that Cobwebs brings them the ineffable pleasure of constant discovery and perpetual adventure, and happiness simply in the business of exploring music together.

Anthony Sargent CBE
General Director
Sage Gateshead

1. Right, let's go! How it all Started

"It might seem an odd name for an orchestra…" So began an article on the occasion of Cobwebs' winning the Gramophone Magazine's 'Music in the Community' award in 2011, ('for an orchestra which has changed lives through music') and so it might do, unless you knew that the first trial run of the idea was a ten-week course called 'Brush the Cobwebs off your music stands and come and play'. The original idea was to encourage those who had played instruments earlier in their lives but let them lapse to take them up again. Since then, two other groups of players have joined: the 'Absolute Beginners', and those who take the opportunity to change to a new instrument. Representatives of each of these groups reflect on their experiences in later chapters.

Cobwebs had its origins in the mid-1990s, when Andy Jackson was appointed as Outreach Worker by a committee of the Northern Sinfonia* (of which Chris Griffiths was, and is, a member) to work in communities in the North East. Chris, now Joint Principal Horn player with the Sinfonia, has thus been a supporter of the Cobweb idea from the very start, and even before. According to Chris, the idea of promoting local outreach in this way was the brainchild of John Summers, the then Chief Executive of Northern Sinfonia, and part of the campaign to promote community music making throughout the North East during the run-up to the building of the Sage, now of course finally built in Gateshead, though several other venues were mooted before its present location was settled on.

The Sinfonia had been committed to outreach in some form from its earliest days. At the very outset of its own life, the founder and first director, Michael Hall, promised the Newcastle Corporation that any surplus made through concerts would be "used to improve the Orchestra and give concerts to the schoolchildren in the city." Thus began a long tradition of work with children and young people throughout the region culminating in the formation of the Young Sinfonia. There had also been a tradition of travelling round small, remote, often rural venues to bring music to people who would not normally have the opportunity to experience the impact of live music events. In the 1970s for example, the annual Lakeland tour included 'informal performances and music workshops in the community, showing something of the potential for extending contact into participation. (Quotes from Bill Griffiths in 'Northern Sinfonia: a Magic of its Own.') Thus we see that the whole Cobwebs project had an antecedent in the philosophy of its 'parent' professional counterpart.

The Sinfonia's Corporate Plan in 1988 declared that "Education is… central to its objective to promote and advance the performance and appreciation of music." The opening of the Sage Gateshead gave the "opportunity to greatly expand the orchestra's work across the full educational sphere from pre-school to Higher education."

Against this promising background then, the scene was set for a new enterprise reaching people of an even wider age group and all abilities. Andy's job as Outreach Worker initially fell into three main categories, the continuation of the educational work in schools, securing engagements for the Sinfonia in local settings, and the new work with adults. Gradually however the emphasis moved towards the latter, Andy feeling that there were lots of people out there who used to play once and needed an opportunity to start again, but who were not always able to commit to regular attendance, or were not confident enough to approach a regular orchestra-and so the idea of the Cobweb orchestra was born.

The first course was held at Annfield Plain, as during his work with local authorities it was Martin Weston, Arts Officer for Derwentside District in North West Durham, who had shown most interest in helping to promote the idea, as "there was no classical music in the area". Martin continues to be hugely supportive of the orchestra and has, we hope, had the satisfaction of seeing some of our major events take place at the Lamplight Theatre in Stanley and in Consett Civic Hall.

The first session took place in October 1995. This is always a nervous moment for any leader. Would enough people come? Would ANYONE come? In the event virtually a full orchestra turned up. Here, three member of that first Cobwebs meeting recall the occasion.

Lesley Wearmouth writes; "I saw a flier at my local pool for a 10 week course to 'Brush the Cobwebs off your music stand.' Although I had never truly given up playing, the opportunity to play in an orchestra was non-existent, so I thought "Why not?" The night I walked into Catchgate library, I knew that Tracy would be there. We had shared the same peripatetic teacher at school and I just had a presentiment that she'd be there- and she was!

An early concert was in a church with a lot of Sinfonia players in support and I remember the highlight for me being a quartet (2clarinets and 2 bassoons). The cheese and wine laid on by the congregation wasn't half bad either."

Tracy recalls her side of the story: "I followed a career in primary school teaching, so I didn't play much for a few years. I found out about Cobwebs because I had seen a flyer in the school staff room. Music was what I'd been missing, and having a Northern Sinfonia player at the helm gave me a feeling that it would be good! I was there on the very first night in Annfield Plain Library, October 1995. It was great to see Lesley again. We'd first met when we joined a wind band at Junior School. The only other surviving players from that first night are Howard (cello) and Jean (violin). Everyone seemed to be so friendly and Andy was so enthusiastic and encouraging. It was only meant to be 10 evening classes to 'blow the cobwebs off your music stands' but everyone wanted it to continue and the name stuck."

Howard Rocke recalls "I hadn't played for 22 years. I didn't even bring my cello over from Ireland when I came to University, but I was encouraged by my children's teacher, Ben Armishaw, to attend a course which was being held at Annfield Plain. I wasn't sure that I'd be able to keep up, there being several peripatetics, not to mention members of the Northern Sinfonia, in the group. However, I finally decided "if you don't try it, you'll never know" and went along. There were lots of people, young and old, everyone with a different story to tell, everyone very friendly. There was no competitiveness, no one-upmanship, instead lots of support, encouragement and the common desire to make music. The Cobwebs concept was born and the experience made me want to play again, even though I had a headache after the first session! It had been a strain sight-reading and remembering how to play all at once. I started practising again and doing exercises to 'get up to speed'. The sheer enjoyment of it had been a very important element in encouraging me to persevere."

Andrew Cottrell, who later (but not much later) shared the soloist's chair with Howard in a memorable performance of Elgar's Cello Concerto, has some nostalgic memories:

"I have been involved with Cobwebs since 1996, very soon after its birth. Since then it has grown immensely and it remains an excellent organisation, chiefly because of its 'all-comers welcome' ethos. Through its weekly groups Cobwebs provides a regular opportunity to make music at a level which most people can manage and enjoy. The weekend events let people attempt larger and varied works which many would otherwise never have dreamed of playing. The participation of professional players from the Northern Sinfonia was really helpful in the early days in getting Cobwebs off the ground. I sometimes feel it is unfortunate they don't join us in the same way nowadays. We still very much welcome input from the few of them who do still help us out as leaders of our workshops or who inspire us as soloists.

Highlights of the earlier years for me include playing the solo part in Elgar's Cello Concerto along with Howard Rocke. I cannot think of another organisation which would give amateurs such an experience. Then there was the first Cobweb concert in The Sage Gateshead's Hall 2 in 2005. The

Sage was then so new and impressive and it was really exciting to be part of it. Various 'Proms in the Park' concerts in Bishop Auckland have also been inspiring, particularly because of the large audiences, notwithstanding concern about risks to some of our instruments from the rain" (and the sun on occasions, Andrew, let's be fair).

The first concert Cobwebs ever gave was in Benfieldside Church, on February 15th 1996 and the group played Schubert's *Rosamunda* and Vaughan Williams' *Greensleeves*. Tracy remembers: "I was so excited to see my family arrive that I had the wrong clarinet in my hand. Luckily Lesley was there to tell me."

Needless to say, the group continued, numbers fluctuating from week to week, but never becoming unviable, though it was not all plain sailing. Lesley recalls that the staff of the library asked the group to put on a concert for them in the Church next door as they had never actually heard them play. "We did, and not one of them turned up to hear us! It was freezing cold and my fingers could hardly move up and down the instrument."

Oh dear, never mind Lesley, you win some...

So, why did they carry on? David Hutton, who joined a little later, has the key:

"After one session packed into a tiny room off Annfield Plain library, I was hooked. The friendly atmosphere, the range of repertoire, from easy to beyond me, from well-known to never heard-of, and the opportunity to play with people who didn't complain if you couldn't keep up or played the wrong notes, these were all contributory factors.

"But the main attraction was the conductor. Andy Jackson is a patient, ever-smiling man who always manages to get the best out of us by encouragement, even when we have been playing badly, and always strives for better things even when we have been playing well. His philosophy includes encouraging professionals and prize-winning players along with beginners and players who haven't played for ages to enjoy music-making together, and though I had played in some excellent school orchestras, I'd not played for some while and had never really played well. Yet, enjoyment is the key to improvement, as I found out."

In addition to being a brilliant and inspiring conductor/director, it was also Andy's organising skills which were vital in keeping this show on the road. From the beginning there were two strands to the activities, the weekly sessions and also the weekend events, the first of which was held at Bishop Auckland Town Hall and was called 'Meet the Sinfonia.' The Bishop Auckland Town Hall (or as it is affectionately known, the BATH) concert has since become a fixture in our timetable, though the involvement of Sinfonia members has reduced since the opening of the Sage, and the Cobwebs' independence, of which more later. The involvement of willing Sinfonia members however has been invaluable and an extra dimension to the 'Cobweb experience' and was vital in those early days. As one member put it, "having a Sinfonia member playing next to you was like getting free tuition and so raised the standard of your playing almost without your realising it."

So this combination of many elements, polishing up old skills, learning new ones, a free and easy atmosphere combined with undoubted hard work and application, the inspiration of a talented leader and the 'leaven' of a few professional players along with the dedication of the members, all these factors have combined to keep the orchestra going- and growing- for nearly 18 years.

The first course turned into a second- there was no way the initial players were going to end it there! More ambitious concerts and events were planned and carried out, and an earlier outline of the Cobwebs' history notes that by April 1996 "the Cobwebs course had turned into an orchestra!" The first newsletter, a single side of A4 typed by Andy, already reports in August 1996 "a spirited performance of Haydn's Symphony No. 104" at Bishop Auckland College in May, and plans for more concerts in Blackhall, and Bishop Auckland Town Hall. It still met on Thursday evenings in Annfield Plain- until it outgrew the venue, and the range of activities it undertook was extraordinary. Andy's hunch had paid off and the mix of musical challenge, food and fun had proved a winner.

The group was off the ground, but how to keep it flying? Andy and Chris used to meet regularly to discuss the way forward. Chris played a Mozart horn concerto in those early concerts, and planned a major event, the 'Mahler Challenge' for early January 1997 (see Chapter 3) But other smaller and more unusual events were planned too. The second newsletter (October 1996) records that: "the Cobweb orchestra has been asked to provide lunchtime music for a seminar at Bishop Auckland on October 28th." Such small events, even now, such as when the Baroque group entertained the U3A in Collingwood College, Durham in Summer 2011, easily go unnoticed and un-recorded, but individuals sign up verbally or more formally, meet to practise, agree dress, programme, travel arrangements, and all to share with others their joy in music making. Other small groups began to spring up either around particular sections of the orchestra or those of different levels of ability, like the Absolute Beginners, or for specific events.

Later newsletters testify that there was on-going discussion around how the 'Cobweb Project' would grow and develop , sometimes by suspending concert performances and all the stress and extra work that entailed, in favour of some workshops concentrating on the 'building blocks of orchestral playing,' with long term supporters Mike Gerrard and Iona Brown from the Sinfonia in attendance.

Numbers continued to increase, even when the 'ringers' (Howard's term for those semi-pros who helped get the group off the ground at the beginning) dropped out. The newsletter, which began in August 1996, was recording a circulation of around 200 by March 1998. News got around- somehow. Here are the recollections of some of those who joined later and have become stalwarts of the Cobwebs family.

Helen Pyburn recalls: "I first heard of the Cobweb orchestra in the year 2000. I worked in Bradley Gardens Nursery at the time, and Cobwebs performed an 'al fresco' evening concert in the gardens. It was August, but the weather was typically British and orchestra and audience had to wrap up warm against the elements. What struck me most was the unavoidably shambolic set-up. They all sat on different height seats, which they had brought with them, with pegs holding the music down, but still it blew off the stands, and yet they seemed to be having fun! I remember that Rosemary was leading, Howard playing cello, Andy was conducting and Jeremy Rowe played a Mozart horn concerto.

There weren't many of them, (and to be truthful some of the music wasn't that brilliant,) but what really hit me was the philosophy of Cobwebs, and I just thought to myself, "I belong there!" So I e-mailed Derek Hobbs and got onto the mailing list and my first event was a Study Day for strings and wind with members of the Northern Sinfonia. This was at Dipton on February 18th 2001 The 2nd violins who were there were too shy to sit sandwiched between Iona Brown and Mike Gerrard at the front, so I sat there- it was fantastic! What an induction! There has been no looking back since then. I gradually built up my attendance to Cobweb events and now it dominates my social life."

Sheila Ryan brought a long family tradition of music making to the Cobwebs table: "As a child I have many happy memories of sharing music with my Mum. She sang a lot to me and taught me songs. When I started going for piano lessons as an 8 year-old, my Mum and I then began to share piano playing and singing. As a teenager I played piano in school and sang, but my school didn't have an orchestra so I was denied the privilege of playing or even of learning an instrument.

When my daughter was 6, she wanted to play recorder and join the school recorder group, and so to keep her company I started playing recorder too. Later she moved on to playing the flute, as well as the piano, and when I saw what pleasure she derived from her lessons (with a Northern Sinfonia player), I soon realised that I had to learn the flute too, so off I went for flute lessons.

It was around that time that I was told my great grandfather had played the flute for a Scottish orchestra, and I was spurred on by that. I also returned to piano lessons and eventually Alison and I entered for the Associated Board duet exams. I found history repeating itself. Here I was deriving pleasure from sharing music with my daughter as I had done with my mother.

As a primary teacher I always played piano for assemblies, concerts, sang with the children, trained a choir, staged musicals and taught recorder groups. I became a member of the Recorder Society and became a member of a recorder quintet, thus improving my recorder skills.

Whilst teaching I was seconded for a year to undertake research into music education, during which time I attended a course in Kodaly music education, which I put into practice when I returned to teaching, and which reinforced my enthusiasm for more pleasurable classroom activities and taught me a lot about the musical capabilities of primary aged children.

It was around this time that one of my recorder playing colleagues mentioned an advert. for a Cobwebs Study Day playing Brahms 2nd symphony at Caedmon Hall, Gateshead under the baton of Alan Fearon. I had never heard of Cobwebs before but together we applied and it was with some fear and trepidation that I sent off for the music and 'dusted the cobwebs off my flute.'

It was at that playing day that I sat beside Lee (Fairlie) and Pauline Holbrook. I very soon realised that I was with two very friendly, supportive and non-critical players. That one very important occasion was the beginning of what has become my lifelong passion for music playing. What had been a daunting day has slowly evolved into a happy and pleasurable part of my life. Strangely enough, all three of us still play the flute when we get together but all of us have changed our main instrument; Lee to the horn, Pauline to oboe and percussion and I to bassoon."

There are many similar stories from people who joined the orchestra as Cobwebs grew and expanded across the north-east and beyond. It is undoubtedly the case that we go from strength to strength in many ways. We improve in standard too, but never, we hope, at the expense of welcoming nervous beginners or returners who feel that they can't keep up. It is probably true to say that an ability to sight-read music is necessary, as one of Andy's strategies for keeping everyone interested and occupied is not to spend too long on any one piece during a rehearsal!

Rehearsal? That is an interesting word. I don't think we actually regard our weekday meetings as 'rehearsals' for anything. Indeed we quite often don't even play the pieces which may be coming up at a weekend workshop or concert. This is partly due to the availability of copies of the music, and also because those who come to weekly meetings don't always play at weekends.

A few Cobweb supporters don't even live in the North of England. Here Sandra Carlile explains how she came to hear of us.

"When I first came to live on the Isle of Wight ten years ago I received a copy of the Sage Magazine. I couldn't understand why this had been sent to me from Cumbria, as I had no connection with Cumbria beyond living in Burnley for twenty years- a little closer than the Isle of Wight. I read through it and saw an advertisement for Folkworks, a weekend of folk music and dancing workshops which I had attended for two or three years. But I had been living in Burnley then, so they didn't have my present address. Reading further I saw an article about the Northern Sinfonia. My husband had done some freelance work with them, but also while we were in Burnley…

Reading on, there appeared a short paragraph saying something called the Cobweb Orchestra was thinking of going to Tuscany in the Summer and was anyone interested? I had never heard of this orchestra but had never been to Tuscany either, so I rang Andrew Forsyth to make further enquiries. Andrew asked my instrument and seemed quite pleased it was Viola. He then asked my name to which I replied: "Sandra Carlile, spelt without an S." After a moment's silence he said: "Would you believe it, our current viola player is Liz Carlile, with Carlile spelt without an S!"

It was 'all go' from there. I have attended all of the Tuscany holidays since (including having a broken arm one year) and enjoyed every minute. They have been wonderful holidays and I think it was just 'meant to be' because I still have no idea why I was sent that original Sage magazine, but whoever sent it, Thank You!'

The combination of opportunities to play during the week or at weekends, in large or small groups, in workshops, 'residentials' (at home or abroad) or concerts means that Cobwebs now has a mailing list of over 1200, and continues with unwaning enthusiasm to bring music to the tentative as well as the talented amateur. In future chapters we look at how the original inspiration continues to blossom in a variety of venues and a variety of styles.

*In the Summer of 2013, the Northern Sinfonia became the "Royal Northern Sinfonia". Whilst acknowledging with delight this accolade, I have retained its former title throughout the text to maintain historical accuracy.

2. New Groups: The Floodgates Open

The First Cumbria Group

The Cobwebs Newsletter of March 1998 carried an advertisement for "musicians living locally in Cumbria and Northumberland" to run orchestral groups in these areas. By August it was announced that "A Cobweb group is starting up soon in Cumbria, funded by Marks and Spencer and Cumbria County Council, with administrative support from Eden Arts… It will be led by Ian Potts with help from Karen West, co-ordinator for COMA (Contemporary Music for Amateurs)."

In January 1999, we hear: "The Cumbria group is now up and running, meeting in the Village Hall at Sandford near Appleby on Thursdays between 7.30 and 9.30. Roughly 20 people turn up and Ian leads them through pieces by Malcolm Arnold, Bizet and Britten, to mention only those at the beginning of the alphabet…"

At the same time, Karen was organising events elsewhere in Cumbria, "for those who find it difficult to get to Sandford on a regular basis". These included a day in Eskdale Village Hall, where in March, Chris Griffiths led a session on Mendelssohn's *1st Symphony* with other members of the Northern Sinfonia also taking part. In the May newsletter, Geoff Braithwaite wrote:

"I still feel as if my feet haven't yet touched the ground since last Saturday's workshop. It was a huge success: everyone enjoyed it immensely, young and old, experienced and inexperienced. (Judy from her position in the audience could tell this just from looking at their faces) and we had a great deal of enthusiastic feedback both on the day and subsequently. I felt sure I would enjoy it since it was the first time I had played my clarinet in an orchestra since leaving school in 1954! But that wasn't the day's record. For an elderly cellist it was the first time he had played for 60 years. He said he was 'a bit rusty and had to keep counting rather hard!'

The remarkable thing was how much both the experienced players and the virtual beginners also enjoyed the day. It speaks volumes for the skills and professionalism of those who led and coached us. It was also remarkable how well balanced we sounded by the end of the day. Mendelssohn's *1st Symphony* was a good choice!"

Ian Potts wrote in the same newsletter:

"Few musicians attend rehearsals accompanied by the sound of distant artillery fire on Warcop ranges or the wind howling across the Cumbrian fells. Fortunately the Cumbrian Cobweb Orchestra was blessed with a quiet evening on the 18th March to celebrate its twentieth rehearsal with a concert for the local people in the hall of the tiny village of Sandford nestled in the foothills of the Pennine hills. Going 'public' for the first time the orchestra played music including Bizet's *Carmen and 'L'Arlesienne,'* Andy Jackson's *Shafto Overture*, Malcolm Arnold's *Trevelyan Suite* and *Amazing Grace*. Very popular with the audience were Jaernefelt's charming Praeludium and Sullivan's *Mikado Overture*.

With two dozen musicians on the playing list even on the 'winteriest' of nights there were never less than a dozen musicians doing their best with Beethoven or running amok with Mozart. The accent is on enjoyment, improving by working on some specific pieces, but also just playing through orchestral and light works to get to know them and just for the fun of it. The orchestra has already spawned a wind quartet that meets in addition to the Thursday evening in Sandford. All instruments, ages and standards are welcome; we will always make sure there is something they can join in with."

Ian also recalled: "There had really been twenty one rehearsals as one memorable evening fifteen intrepid members made the three-hour round trip to Stanley to join members of the Annfield Plain group and delight in the full sound of Sibelius' *Karelia Suite* and Benjamin Britten's *Soirees Musicales*." This is a tradition which continues to this day, as we now virtually expect to see Sue and often Andrew, over from Kirby Stephen and Weasdale to swell our numbers in Consett.

By the beginning of 2000, Ian reported that the group was devoting "serious (not that we were ever that serious) study to a number of pieces. In particular, Eric Coates' *Three Bears Suite* proved tricky but great fun. Especially enjoyable was our joint rehearsal with the Durham group one Saturday in October. Having more strings allowed us to have a proper go at Dvorak's *Eighth* and Tchaikovsky's *'Romeo and Juliet'* again. We all retired to the Sandford Arms for lunch and drinks while the Cumbria group's wind quartet entertained. The last rehearsal before Christmas included the premiere of our bassoonist Dick Barlow's *'Cobweb March'*, complete with lyrics."

For one member of the Tebay orchestra, its advent came in the nick of time. Here is Sheila Blackwell's story from the cello ranks.

"I joined the Cobweb orchestra the year I retired. I had finished playing in the Sedbergh School orchestra (where I had worked) and it seemed a good time to start somewhere new. My introduction was with Dr. Michael Flindt who took me along the first time. Although I had done my Grade 5 exams, my sight-reading was not good and I found everything difficult and very exposed. Then Rosemary arrived, and between us we soldiered on, depending on each other as she could count and I could cope with the notes! So we became a team, a crazy team, on the first (and only!) desk in those days. 2003 saw us both off on the Tuscany trip, a wonderful week which hooked us both totally on the Cobweb experience for life. Lessons continued and Tuesday nights at Tebay became a vital part of the improvement process, though concerts were never very comfortable unless we had a few good players from the Other Side to join us". [We presume she means the Pennines, not the Spirit World!]

"The orchestra means so much to so many people, not only for the experience of playing wonderful and sometimes difficult music. Aided by the gifted players who help us all along with such good grace and humour, the Study Days at our various towns contribute a lot to improving our playing, and also in forming friendships with people from other groups. There is great joy in mastering a seemingly impossible work, or at least in not getting totally lost and playing if not all the notes then a great many more than previously!"

These reminiscences highlight several features which have become typical of Cobweb events; the sharing of musical enjoyment across groups, the integral importance of food ("Food and Music always go Together" to quote a ditty composed by our Director), and the inspiration our activities give to those individuals blessed with the talent for composition, especially when they realise they have an opportunity to hear their efforts performed.

The Northumberland Group

Meanwhile, in Autumn 1999 in Northumberland, a third group was coming into being. A concert was held in Newbiggin Sports and Leisure Centre in September, where, under the baton of Baldur Bronnimann, the existing Cobweb Orchestra plus players from the Sinfonia played Mozart's *Symphony No. 40* and Tchaikovsky's 5th. Bryan Jackson recalls the conductor's list of priorities: "Passion, counting, rhythm and finally notes. I like that man!" After this inspiring send-off, one member said that he was about to begin lessons again after a forty year break, and so the Northumberland group was born. It met initially in Woodhorn Church, soon moving to the Colliery museum. As leader Derek Hobbs said: "What the room lacks in atmosphere and helpful acoustics, it makes up for in warmth". His fears that potential recruits may have been scared off by the high standard reached in the concert proved unfounded and 40 players turned out, a full complement save for a bassoon. Derek's own talents as a composer/arranger were often used to fill out extra parts, to accord with the Cobweb principle that no-one should be left sitting doing nothing for too long. A debut concert was planned for Easter 2000.

Sheila Ryan also recalls playing with the Northumberland group, and soon filled the bassoon shaped gap in their ranks.

"As soon as the Northumberland Cobwebs group was established at Woodhorn Church, (later it moved to Woodhorn itself followed by Newbiggin Sports Centre and now Morpeth,) I was hooked. Initially I played in the flute section and found Derek Hobbs such an encouraging conductor, just as David Hutton was after him. Whilst playing in my recorder group I started playing bass recorder. I quickly realised that I loved playing bass and decided I would like to take up a bass instrument, but which one? I pondered for a long time and I knew I just had to go for it- the bassoon!"

The "Second Wave"
As long as the Cobwebs association with the Sinfonia/Sage continued we were not able to expand beyond 3 groups, but as soon as we went independent in 2007 the flood gates opened and the simmering demand for more could be met. New groups sprang up in Dalston, Cumbria, in Middlesbrough, later in York, the Sage and most recently in Spennymoor, a group which is growing and thriving under the leadership of Greg Pullen.

The Dalston Group
Since the early days of Cobwebs, a number of players from North Cumbria had been supporting the big events held at weekends, but the nearest weekly group was almost 40 miles away at Tebay and met the same night as the City of Carlisle Orchestra.

One of these players was Peter Wood, who had been on some conducting workshops run for Cobwebs by Alistair

Credit: The Cumberland News, Carlisle

Dawes. Peter was keen to continue to conduct but had no orchestra! With a little persuasion from Andy Jackson, he agreed to start a new Cobweb group in North Cumbria.

Peter and his wife Ruth along with Julie Ratcliffe spent many hours looking for a suitable venue, identifying some prospective players, and arranging newspaper and radio publicity and posters to promote the new group.

Dalston was chosen as the venue, having a good hall, being only five miles from the M6 and west of Carlisle, it was considered more likely to attract players from Wigton and Cockermouth in West Cumbria. A workshop with Peter on Haydn's *Clock Symphony* was arranged for Saturday 16 February 2008 and this attracted 25 potential members for the new group, as well as a number of players from the other Cobweb groups.

The first rehearsal for the new group, in one of the smaller back rooms at Dalston's Victory Hall, was held on Monday 25 February 2008 and was attended by 28 players. The group met fortnightly, and Cumberland Building Society made a contribution to the group's initial costs.

Dalston soon became a venue for big events, hosting a workshop on (yet again) Mahler's *First Symphony* within two months of the group starting. In March 2009 the Dalston Group arranged a ceilidh in the Dalston Victory Hall with the Cobwebs Ceilidh Band which raised over £600 for Cobwebs.

In April 2010 the group moved into the main hall at Dalston, and changed from a fortnightly group to meeting weekly. The change from fortnightly to weekly rehearsals did initially see a small reduction in the number of players each week as would be expected with busy people! However the group continues to attract new and enthusiastic players.

As the Dalston group approaches its fifth anniversary, it is in good health and has regular players for all sections of the orchestra (except percussion). In addition, two of the initial flute players, Julie Ratcliffe and Terry Mullet, now playing French horn and trombone respectively, took advantage of the Cobwebs instrument bank to switch instruments, leaving the crowded flute section for pastures new.

The Teesside Group

This group began as a weekly session but had to move to meeting fortnightly in order to try and make ends meet. It is good to report that they now meet weekly again. It met under the baton, initially of Rebecca Pedlow and then of Clare Barker, now Clare Carr, a longstanding Cobweb French horn player familiar with the ethos and expectations of the Cobweb project. To begin with the little group met (rather intimidatingly) in a corner of the main Middlesbrough Town Hall or else down in the crypt, as the Middlesbrough council were eager to encourage the arts in the area. Later they moved to the much cosier setting of a church hall in Billingham, where Clare continues to challenge and coax the best from the group. Clare recalls her first experience of Cobwebs:

"The first time I came across the Cobweb orchestra was when the Harelaw group were doing a concert at my younger sister's school, and I was invited to play French horn. I had a great time and found the group members very friendly and welcoming. After finishing my degree and completing a year of professional training in 2003, I returned home to find that I was missing the orchestras and music groups in which I had been involved whilst still at school. I remembered Cobwebs, gave it a try and, finding good company, satisfying music and lots of fun, decided to stick around! Having "dabbled" in a bit of conducting over the past couple of years with the ever tolerant and supportive Guinea Pig orchestra, and at occasional Harelaw group rehearsals, I joined the Leaders' group and was delighted to be given the opportunity to run the Beginners' Course."

Yes, another type of group! Cobwebs occasionally offers Beginners' Days, or courses, for those who need that gentle easing in to playing again, or for the first time, in an orchestra, always a rather daunting, if exciting experience initially.

Interestingly an afternoon group was also created at the Sage Gateshead, catering for those who prefer a daytime meeting, and it has gone from strength to strength, often performing to the general public in the foyer informally as well as joining in workshops and performances in the big halls. Few would have aspired or dared even to contemplate such heights when they started. One member said after taking part in a performance of the Dvorak cello concerto, with 'our own' Alice Jones as soloist: "I never in this world imagined I would be doing this!" Our new relationship with the Sage is a nice example of walking away as an offspring and returning as a friend.

The Sage Group
Alan Verheyden writes:

"The Sage Cobweb orchestra currently (March 2013) attracts a gathering of between forty and fifty players each week. Until recently numbers varied so much that Andy never knew when he started rehearsing a piece of music whether or not the term would end with the same players. What a task he has in trying to cater for the wide range of ability that our group has within it.

As numbers have grown in the last few months we have had to reflect on the capacity of the room we use and think about creating another smaller group in a neighbouring room. As yet Andy has not come up with the criteria for sorting us into two groups but hopefully it will not be a matter of sheep and goats! Having said this, there have been people who have come along to a few sessions and found the music a little too challenging, so we never saw them again. As numbers continue to grow we need constantly to look into how we retain the beginners / intermediate players while challenging the more advanced.

In common with most groups there are the regular stalwarts who ensure that each week the chairs, stands, music folders, money collection and timps are all in place. Yes, TIMPS! We are so fortunate to have access to these at the Sage. Recently a Grade 8 timpanist came along to play with us. Access to a double bass has also given the opportunity to one of our young violinists to take up the instrument with minimum transportation problems, unlike our lead cellist who has two buses to catch!

Not only do we enjoy the privilege of being able to play in such a splendid venue, we have the added bonus of being able to eat and drink in the Sage. Cobweb member often meet for lunch in the café before our session and when music making is over groups relax and socialise, many enjoying the delights on offer in the coffee shop. A great hit for many months was 'Anthony's Tart of the Week.' We were never quite sure if this was baked personally by Anthony Sargent, the Sage Director!" Apparently the Sage's chef is also called Anthony, but they enjoy the regular misunderstanding.

The York group
Our most distant and adventurous challenge was to set up a group in York. This was largely because of the long association of Catherine Shackell, née Holbrook, with Cobwebs through her mother Pauline's membership and her own interest in music from an early age. Here, Pauline explores the origins of the venture:

"In 2006 Andy approached Catherine and invited her to start a Cobweb group in York. As a young person, Catherine had been associated with the Cobweb enterprise through work experience with Andy, with a view to a later career as a professional musician and was very supportive of the idea of encouraging people who had once played instruments but had lost the habit, back into the world of music. She had even contributed to the enterprise by trawling through Groves and other sources looking for music suitable for small orchestras, and played her bassoon in the orchestra along with her mother Pauline, who played the flute, then percussion, then oboe.

Catherine went on to fulfil her ambition and gained a degree in music and an MA in Community Music at York. Whilst studying she had maintained her links with Cobwebs through composition, performance and occasional conducting, so starting a new group in York seemed a natural progression for her. After researching the viability of such a venture, and looking around for venues, and an advertising campaign, Catherine launched the York group early in 2008 with a 'Come and Play' study day on Mozart's Haffner Symphony at Earswick Village Hall, supported by members from other existing Cobweb groups. On that day there were 40 players present, with a third of the orchestra playing celli."

Jim Hoggett takes up the story:

"After its launch, with the first regular group meeting on 21st February 2008, the new orchestra rapidly gained a solid local membership base, many of whom fitted the typical Cobweb stereotype - instruments left in cupboards for years, with little or no hope that they would ever be played again. Rehearsals in the first year covered a diverse range of smaller and larger works from the Cobweb library, as well as music arranged and sourced by Catherine. The orchestra grew in size, enthusiasm and (we hoped!) quality. The first anniversary was celebrated by the group hosting its first Cobweb concert in Haxby and Wigginton Methodist Church Hall, where the orchestra played Purcell's *Abdelazar*, Moze's *Witches on a Trip to Naples* and other Cobweb favourites, followed by a dance performance by young members of a local youth theatre.

It had become clear over the first year or so that one of the prices of success was that the orchestra no longer fitted comfortably in the original premises, so it moved in Autumn 2009 to New Earswick Village Hall which was its home for the next 3 years. The repertoire covered a wide span from early classical and baroque to forays into romantic music, (Brahms, Dvorak,) plus Grieg, Elgar, and local composer, Baines, all within the first 12 months. A "Russian Roots" day in Haxby in January 2010 was a great success. Schubert is a favourite for many, so the choice of his 5th *Symphony*, with Mozart's *Impresario Overture*, was a popular choice for the second Cobweb concert hosted by the group in The Mount School in March 2010.

Cobweb groups are very used to rehearsing and giving concerts in Church and Town Halls – some better than others acoustically and in terms of available facilities. York is fortunate in having access to the Lyons Concert Hall (part of the University's Music Department), which is a great performance venue. Two events are memorable in the local Cobweb history: Dvorak's magical 9th *New World Symphony* in February 2011 and Schubert's *C major Symphony*, combined with Chopin's 1st *Piano Concerto* with Emily Murray as soloist in March 2012. It is hard to express the pleasure and sense of achievement that amateur musicians, not least Cobwebbers, get from taking on these major awe-inspiring works.

The group has also hosted happy and typical 'food-and-music' Cobweb activities such as the Cabaret Tea Party in December 2011, and has participated in York-based events such as the open air Peace Festival in September 2011. Recorded for posterity (for better or worse!) on a hot summer's evening in 2012, the York Cobweb group's playing of Mozart's *Symphony 41* was featured in a publicity film clip by Making Music, the national umbrella organisation for amateur music, along with enthusiastic sound-bites about the joys of Cobwebbing from its players.

As a relatively new group in the Cobweb organisation, it took a little time to establish participation in other group's activities and Cobweb residentials, but that now seems to have become much more part of the pattern of quite a few of the members' musical lives. There also seems to be a perception (on the part of other groups also) that York is a little geographically remote from the Cobweb heartland, but this perception is more imagined than real as North-South road and rail connections are very good, and less at the mercy of the weather than some!

Sadly, in the late summer of 2012, Catherine decided that she was no longer able to work within the organisation or to lead the York group. The York Cobweb group continued to meet in autumn 2012 with limited numbers under the leadership of Jonathan Brigg, who had previously stood in for Catherine, and had conducted a Cobweb Study Day of Borodin's 2nd *Symphony* in Carperby near Richmond in July 2012. At the start of 2013, the York Cobweb group moved to new premises at the Steiner School and on a new night, now Wednesdays. The initial come-and-try-it "Cobweb and Curry" evening (an idea to recommend to all groups!) attracted about 20 new participants, and since then numbers have grown strongly, forming a well-balanced orchestra with secure and healthy numbers, under the baton of our enthusiastic and inspiring conductor. Initial fears that the hall would be too large have proved unfounded. The proximity of good pubs adds to the pleasures of the later evening, and one of the landlords is very generous with his (free!) cheese and biscuits.

The first experience of many new members of the group to the activities of the wider Cobweb organisation was a study day on the *Rite of Spring* in Haxby Memorial Hall in February 2013. All credit to Andy for making the apparently impossible both possible and approachable. Undeterred by its introduction to the challenges of additive rhythms, the York group turned out in force at this year's Big Play event in Middlesbrough and also the Sedbergh residential, where an apprehensive group of York players embraced the Cobweb ethos by attempting performances at the Saturday night concert! With such an enthusiastic, youthful and expanding bunch of players, the future of the York group looks secure."

The Spennymoor Group
By Helen Mills

"A new group sprung up in Spennymoor in 2011 led by professional cellist and composer, Greg Pullen. I attended the initial meeting as one of the many flutes that typically arrive in their droves. There was, of course, a good turn-out of cellos and two basses but we could do with more upper strings. Brass and woodwind were represented, we had two trumpets- now three. We lose a horn when founder member Lee Fairlie retires and moves away taking her husband too, David, a cellist. (Watch this space for Cobwebs Manchester!)

I am a typical Cobwebber. I learnt the piano to Grade 6 and Theory to Grade 8, then took up the flute at secondary school in Chester, without learning scales and without taking exams. I left my flute at home when I went to Newcastle University. Now after twenty five years and three children later I am having some flute lessons because I discovered Cobwebs when I joined Durham Scratch choir and met Andy Jackson and Liz Carlile. My debut was at Middlesbrough Town hall and along came the kids to make instruments out of hosepipe and plastic bottles, a workshop with Catherine Holbrook and David Hutton. Somewhere there is a photo in the Middlesbrough Gazette of myself and fellow new Cobwebber Ray Dominy (trumpet) proudly smiling, showing our shiny instruments."

In addition to the geographical groups, other small ensembles have grown up catering for sectional interests, (the string and wind ensembles), and the groups which cater for particular interests such as the Composers and Arrangers' group, with their attendant "Guinea-pig orchestra", mentioned above by Clare, and the Conductors', later the Leaders' group. Andy soon came to realise that he needed to communicate that there was more to leading a community orchestra like ours than merely conducting it in a sympathetic way. This group was created as a crash course in how to help a community music group prosper, and to create good music without frightening people away.

The Conductors' Group, the Leaders' Group and 'Composers and Arrangers'
David Hutton recalls:

"One night Andy asked if any of us would like to have a go at composing, conducting, arranging, or anything else new. Each of these seemed an impossible aspiration, out of reach of most of us, and we needed quite a bit of encouragement, which Andy, in his quiet friendly way, was always free with. At first some of us had a go at conducting small pieces which the orchestra knew, and we followed them, and then sometimes they actually followed us too! Then ten of us joined in a marathon session in Bishop Auckland Town Hall to conduct Beethoven's *Fifth*. Wow! It was like a relay race - literally passing the baton from one to another, and how exhilarating it was for us all.

But we needed more than just enthusiasm for this skill to blossom - it needed practice and coaching. This was provided by the Conductors' Group, less amorphous than most of the groups, since we had to aim at putting ourselves in front of an orchestra rather than just joining in the middle of the back row. We had instruction, coaching and practice, not only from Andy, but also from the conductors at Covent Garden and the Northern Sinfonia, no less, each with their own experience and views, but sharing the desire to encourage us. So we studied scores and we struggled with doing three or more things at once, and we had the invaluable support of the GPO - the Guinea Pig Orchestra. That's right, they were the "guinea pigs" who came along free to be experimented on while we practised our emerging craft on them. How lucky we were to be given not just the coaching but the practical experience.

This was later followed by the Leaders' Group (see below) so that we could understand the many other demands on the conductor of a weekly group besides "waving the baton." So when Derek Hobbs decided that he wanted to finish leading the Newbiggin group (which true to Cobweb form has rehearsed in many Northumberland venues,) Andy approached me to take over the job. I was reluctant to follow such an inspiring leader as Derek, but eventually agreed as the need was obvious, and spent two enjoyable years with them, before also having to pass on the baton, this time to Lizelle Kirby, who had also gained from, and contributed much to, the Conductors', Leaders' and also the Composers' and Arrangers' groups.

The GPO also supported the work of several of us who aspired to be Composers and Arrangers, a group which started about the same time as the Conductors. The results of these small beginnings have blossomed enormously with many players showing us what they can compose, and others of us arranging pieces to be played by an orchestra whose members could include saxophones or could number 6 flutes and no second violins.

Andy was familiar with the demands of a group whose members were not always able to attend every week, and which could be joined by unexpected others (like an accordion player, yes it did happen!) or in amazing combinations or numbers. At our 10th birthday celebrations in Hexham for example, we had 14 clarinets. So Andy had already been writing flexible arrangements to suit a core of just a few essential players and expandable to include almost any player who could join in. And while many of our arrangements aspired to this approach, we as players were also being encouraged to be flexible - those many flautists could just as well play from a violin part, and clarinettists could even read from a viola part with a bit of practice."

Peter Wood wrote the following piece for one of our newsletters:

Behind the Scenes: The Leaders' Group

"As the number of Cobwebs groups has grown, so has their diversity. The instrumental make-up of each group, the number of players, their ability and the music played is individual to each of them. However, they all promote the same Cobweb ethos. In the past, leaders have discussed the ethos and its practical application to ensure that each group provides enjoyable, all inclusive rehearsals where players leave at the end of the evening wanting to come back and play again.

With the groups spread over a wide area, it is difficult to keep in touch with each group's development and its activities. To overcome this, the leaders try to meet quarterly with Andy Jackson to ensure continued focus on the ethos, to share information about their individual groups and to discuss future events. Typical items have included: Sharing Ideas: what worked with your group? What wasn't so good? Help with problems: we haven't got any cellos/brass, so what can we play without them and how can we get some? Weekly attendances: growing/declining - why? Choice of Music: What is your group playing at the moment? Where did you get the music from? Can we borrow it? Arrangements for forthcoming events; e.g. Core works that each group should try to look at, with a view to playing together in a future joint event, e.g. Bizet's *Symphony in C*, and Elgar's *Enigma Variations*. And last but not least, Group Leader exchanges, encouraging leaders to swap groups for an evening and identifying new leaders, plus further training opportunities for existing leaders."

Little do most of us realise the background work and thought which goes into making our one musical evening a week, or the occasional weekend workshop, so enjoyable and inspiring!

As an example of the proliferation of the smaller specialist instrumental groups, here is a sample weekend from October 2009.

Saturday 17th and Sunday 18th: An Ensembles weekend: 2 days of group activity across the Northern Counties.

Saturday:	**Flutes**	Wylam	2pm – 5pm
	Clarinets	Haltwhistle	11am – 4pm
	Oboes and Bassoons	Tebay	2pm – 5pm
	Brass	Dipton	2pm – 5pm
	Baroque Group	Earswick Village Hall Nr. York	2pm – 5pm
Sunday:	**Ceilidh Band**	Wylam	10am – 1pm
	Conductors with GPO	Wylam	2pm – 5pm

These small instrumental groups enable members to concentrate on improving their own technique and also give the opportunity to explore another part of the repertoire. The wind and brass section have benefitted from the involvement of both Stephen Reay (Bassoon, Northern Sinfonia) who has accompanied us to Tuscany twice, and Chris Griffiths.

Tracy Reed recalls the highlights for her.

Working with Professionals: Wind Ensembles with Chris Griffiths.

"I can't decide which wind ensemble piece with Chris is my favourite because I've loved them all. Mozart's *Gran Partita* was performed at Toby's birthday party at the Sage. We found ourselves performing to an audience when we assumed we were to be "background" music. I loved Wagner's *Siegfried Idyll* at the Sage too, although the recording includes my very loud clarinet squeak, never to be forgotten! Another favourite has to be the Dvorak *Wind Serenade*, which we performed at Bishop Auckland Town Hall in February 2012; it has the most glorious clarinet moments in the second movement."

The Quintessentials Wind Quintet.

"When Marj Baillie joined Cobwebs on flute, she asked if I would like to be in a wind quintet, along with fellow Cobwebbers Jeremy Rowe on horn and Catherine Worsley on bassoon. It was Catherine's idea to call ourselves The Quintessentials, and we would often have our own slot in a Cobweb concert. Catherine even arranged music especially for us: Prokofiev's '*Romeo and Juliet*' and a Christmas medley. Our oboist left, and we were joined by another Cobwebber, Liz Challand. The most memorable event has to be playing Andy Jackson's arrangement of Handel's *Water Music* in June 2002. The orchestra played the first and third suites and the quintet played the middle suite on a boat moving down the River Wear in Sunderland.

It wasn't long after that when Catherine died. The quintet had to play in a concert without her that very night. Ian Dawson, son of our percussionist, Doug, replaced Catherine. That was the hardest concert I ever had to do. We had made a recording of the *Water Music* in case there were problems on the boat, so at least we have something to remind us of Catherine's wonderful playing. I didn't know that the CD would be played at her funeral. It was so sad. I still think of her whenever we play Handel. It's a shame that the quintet no longer meets but I have some very fond memories and I learnt such a lot about playing in a chamber ensemble."

The TRIL Clarinet quartet.

"Ian Potts asked if I would play in a clarinet quartet in a concert in Appleby Public Hall in April 2008, organised by the Rotary Club to raise money for a music award at the Grammar School. Ian came up with a clever name for us: TRIL (Tracy, Ruth, Ian, Lesley!) We really enjoyed the music, including *'Summertime'* and the *St. Louis Blues*. We got to perform as a group again a few months later as part of a concert organised by and featuring Mike Cave on the flute, in aid of the British Heart Foundation."

Other wind groups sprang up from time to time. We were often blessed with large numbers of flutes, far beyond what the usual orchestra would tolerate. In 2007 indeed, Andy wrote a clarinet choir and a flute choir into the score of the *Gospel Requiem*. A Flute Day at Woodhorn Colliery gave flute players (forty of them!) the opportunity to "work intensively without being distracted by string, reed or brass players". Some dozen of them decided to meet monthly to play through the flute repertoire.

The reed, flautists and horn players did however get together in November 2003 to benefit from a day's workshop with the Aurora Ensemble where they took part in "big ensembles, small ensembles, single instrument workshop workshops and problem solving sessions".

In Autumn 2008, a frustrated Lesley Wearmouth announced that after "many years hoping someone else would organise a day for clarinets, John Harling and I have decided to organise one this year".

Cello players, similarly, benefitted from days with Jeanette Mountain of the Sinfonia, and string players as a whole from working with Iona Brown, and Bradley Creswick, and it was out of these occasional group meetings that the Ensembles days we enjoy today evolved.

One grouping that was rather more short-lived was the **Music by Heart** group. This began in late 2001. Andy wrote that Isaac Stern is quoted as saying: "Learning music by reading is like making love by mail." [We could say today 'on line'] Despite Andy's enthusiasm for being "free of the worry about what the notes are, and being able to concentrate on sound expression, ensemble, style and other subtle things" the group, after several sessions around the region and a few performances, such as at the Kielder Residential weekend, has rather petered out. Perhaps it is in the nature of classical musicians to be rather too dependent on "the dots" and, let's face it, perhaps in general too old to be comfortable playing without music. Andy mused about the progress of the group in March 2003. "It has been an interesting, challenging, puzzling and upbeat series of meetings so far. Methods of memorisation used seem to vary hugely between individuals but few seem unable to memorise at all, and some, especially children, seem to be very good at it." David Hutton confesses that he found it "difficult to remember accurately what I was supposed to be playing. I could play something which fitted well but was not necessarily what had been written by the composer." So for David it was in danger of becoming an Improvisation Group!

One of the most successful Music by Heart events was deemed to be a performance of a movement from an early Mozart symphony in Morpeth in June 2005. "Not only did we remember (almost) all the notes, we also managed to do without a conductor and stood to play, which made for greater communication between players and a very lively rendition which was hugely enjoyed by those listening."

The Cabaret Group

The Cabaret Ensemble started as a group of players who signed up to accompany some poems written by Ramsey Rutherford, the brother of a member of the Singing from Scratch Choir, which Andy set to music. He put the usual request out for 'anyone interested' and a strange assortment of players came forward including 3 violas, and a percussionist but no 'cello or bass instrument. The event took place, cabaret style, with poetry readings interspersed with music, at the Gala Theatre in Durham. It was then taken to London, where Ramsey had had professional friends and colleagues and also Lanchester.

Later the group was revived as a 'one instrument to a part' group often including a guitar, and usually plays in small venues like hotels or in people's houses. Another early group "gig" was in April

2003 when they played an arrangement of music by the "little Count" Borulawski, who had travelled around Europe and then retired to Durham in the early 19th century. There was also a Billie Holliday evening at Bishop Auckland Town Hall in December 2004 with Bridie Jackson.

Tracy again:

"It seemed a long time before the Cabaret Group formed again, with different Cobwebbers and a bigger emphasis on what we would wear! A joint concert with the North East recorder Orchestra at the Sage in September 2011 gave us the chance to even get changed in the interval! The Cabaret Ensemble have been booked to perform at private functions, including my Dad's surprise 70th birthday party, Anita's Mum and Bob's wedding anniversary party, and the Haltwhistle Walking Festival. I just love the jazzy music, especially when the two clarinets are playing together. *La Mer, Lady Sings the Blues, I who have Nothing, Sunny Afternoon, Sally, Mood Indigo...*"

The Baroque Group

The Baroque group has flourished under the direction of Toby Lipman, ably assisted by Elizabeth Beer and has reached a high standard of performance in their concerts, through regular practice every Tuesday evening. It is mainly a string orchestra, with a penchant for Vivaldi and Corelli violin concertos, with occasional "visiting" Cobweb soloists on flute, oboe, organ or trumpet, as we sample the works of Albinoni, Handel and Bach. The experience of playing in this group is rather like singing in a madrigal group, in that there are usually no more than two instruments to a part, (often only one) so your contribution matters and is heard! Intonation and the art of listening and blending are greatly enhanced, as is the skill of reading from cramped handwritten scores with some unaccustomed conventions, like splitting bars between lines and the custom of putting a 'flat' sign in order to change a note from 'sharp' to 'natural.' Not to mention Toby's handy hints on trying to get as close as possible to the Baroque style, (no vibrato!) albeit on modern instruments.

After a concert for the University of the 3rd Age (U3A) in the Summer of 2010, the conference organiser wrote in his letter of appreciation -"Thank you for your wonderful performance. The Cobweb orchestra pulled us into its web," and after a concert as the opening event of the St Giles' Church Durham's 900th anniversary Flower Festival in 2012, the Vicar declared that he had been "deluged with beauty." (Indeed, hankies were spotted in the audience during the slow movement of the Albinoni *Oboe Concerto*.) The group were asked to play again in 2013, a sure sign of success!

A fellow Cobweb member wrote after a concert in the 2012 Sedbergh Festival: "Last night I was very proud to be a member of the Cobweb Orchestra. Our Baroque Ensemble were outstanding, the oboe concerto was delightful with very sensitive playing by all involved. The double violin concerto was a joy and the ensemble as a whole was brilliant. Feedback from other people who attended was "What a wonderful concert!"

Toby Lipman, who also leads the main Cobweb Orchestra, relates how he came to be playing with the Cobwebs:

"I started to learn the violin as an eight year old at the Royal Grammar School, Newcastle upon Tyne, and found it pretty hard going at first. My father, to encourage me, played recordings of famous violin concertos, and a recording that took my fancy from the beginning was by Isaac Stern, of the Mendelssohn and Bruch concertos. He conceded that the Bruch was "quite good for modern music" (yes, he did say that) but his favourite, and mine, was the Mendelssohn.

At this stage I was still playing "A Tune a Day" and struggling with Grade One pieces, but I borrowed the music from the library anyway, because it was in E Minor, which had only one sharp, and therefore should be fairly straightforward. The Bruch, in G Minor, had 2 flats, a much more dubious proposition at that stage.

I put the violin part on my stand and goggled at it. It seemed to be quite a bit trickier than I had anticipated, although I could at least scratch out one or two of the famous tunes - and that was fantastic - the first "real" music that I had ever played. It hooked me on the violin and ignited an ambition, which has always lurked in the back of my mind, to learn the piece and one day play it with a piano accompaniment in place of the orchestra. But I never found a pianist willing to play the orchestral reduction.

Then I discovered the Cobweb orchestra. Since I joined it I have found great friends to make music with-not only orchestral, but string quartets, other chamber music, the Baroque Ensemble. I've had the opportunity to perform concertos by baroque composers such as Vivaldi, Corelli, Handel, but until now not romantic concertos such as the Mendelssohn. On June 26th I will be sixty, and the Cobweb orchestra is giving me the best birthday present I could imagine: the chance to attempt the Mendelssohn concerto with an orchestra in the Barbour Room at the Sage Gateshead."

Another fairytale come true!

3. Repertoire: "We're playing WHAT?"

If anyone in Cobwebs imagined that the challenging symphony they played at a workshop the other weekend was something the orchestra had worked up to over the years, think again!

As soon as the trial 10-week course was completed and the decision made to keep going, ambitious works were attempted. Andy begins the first newsletter in August 1996:

"It seems a very long time since that spirited performance of Haydn's *104th (symphony)* at Bishop Auckland College in May." He ends the same newsletter:

"AND Chris Griffiths is hoping to conduct a performance of Mahler's *1st* in Alnwick next January, using amateur players and musicians from the Northern Sinfonia."

Did it go ahead? Of course it did! Chris recalls certain difficulties he faced in putting this event on, with some doubts expressed as to whether it would really work, but he also remembers the support and determination of others to make it happen. Chris himself should take much credit as it was his brainchild to mount the event and he took on much of the fundraising to enable it to take place. Chris pays tribute especially to the then Manager of Alnwick Playhouse who helped secure the final tranche of money needed to secure the event. (Indeed Chris recalls that so thrilled was he when this offer was made during the interval of a Sinfonia concert that he was late back on stage for the second half, inevitably receiving a personal round of applause as he scuttled back into the hall!) In the end the concert was a great success, with participation of players from Northallerton to Glasgow, ex-players from the Northern Junior Phil., including Bryan Jackson, who became a regular Cowebs stalwart, and founder members of the Young Sinfonia, John Pratt (horn) and Rosie Hillier-Jenkins (oboe).

John Hawkes recalls his rather surprising, but very typical introduction to the ways of Cobwebs:

"My first encounter with the Cobwebs was in January 1997 at the 'Mahler 1 Challenge' at Alnwick Playhouse with Chris Griffiths conducting and which included players from the Cobwebs, the Northern Sinfonia and the Young Sinfonia. No sooner had I arrived than a cor anglais was thrust into my hand. The fact that I had never played one before seemed not to matter one jot, the main reasoning seemed to be that I was deemed old enough to take reasonable care of it! Andy Jackson was there and I seem to remember that one of his roles was to prepare easier parts for players if required."

Incidentally, as Peter Wood recalls elsewhere, Mahler's *First Symphony* was the subject of the first workshop hosted by the fledgling Dalston group in 2008. It is obviously felt to be a work which is challenging- but not too challenging, very rewarding, memorable- and great fun. Just as well we didn't know its nickname "The Titan!"

Here lies a clue as to the complexities of choosing a repertoire for an orchestra like ours, from the idealistic "What would we like to play?" to the more practical "What can the band play that they are capable of tackling without disappointment?" and "What will stretch the better players without frustrating the more limited?" to the very basic "Where can we get the music for that?" This unenviable task falls mostly to Andy.

Various themes have been adopted through the years, such as the "Year of Loud Music", 400 Years of English Music, and the Month of the Symphonies, (Mozart, Schumann, Shostakovich, Tchaikovsky). Many of us have learnt for the first time, and fallen in love with, the Cesar Franck symphony, delighted in Dvorak, been exasperated by Elgar (more difficult than we imagined) and then there was that famous day when we played all Beethoven's symphonies in one day in Middlesbrough Town Hall. More recently Andy has introduced us to several lesser known works like the Rachmaninov, and Borodin's 2nd, plus most recently, in 2012, a symphony by Samuel Coleridge

Taylor. Mozart and Haydn's great works provide the opportunity for sensitivity and exactitude, while the wonderful wide vistas of Sibelius satisfy the romantic in us.

Over the years we have been lucky enough to play various concertos, from individual movements with some outstanding soloists who are pupils of local teachers, to whole works with some brilliant soloists. Chris Griffiths, who was, of course with us from the start, played a Mozart Horn concerto in Autumn 1996. Boriana Nakeva played the ever popular Mendelssohn *Violin Concerto* in 2000, and is remembered for spending time carefully tuning every string instrument in the orchestra herself. Jo Sampson wrote on the back of her programme "Very fine performance. She was obviously too good for us!" Boriana was probably not alone in that, but it is very inspiring for us to have excellent soloists, some of whom, like Min-Jin Kim, are happy to brush up their performance techniques with us, by using us as a rehearsal opportunity. Iona Brown of the Northern Sinfonia gave a performance of the Bruch *Violin Concerto* which was a memorable favourite of Brian Tanner in his early days as a Cobwebber, (repeated in 2013) and he himself accomplished a "heart's desire" by playing the Saint-Saëns *Organ Symphony* in the hall of Sedbergh School with the orchestra.

Recently we have had the good fortune to play cello works with Alice Jones, who played in the orchestra with us before going to train as a soloist in London. With Alice we have played the Elgar *Cello Concerto*, always a memorable and moving experience, and a *Concertino* written for her by our own John Hawkes. Helen Pyburn has written a *Horn Concerto* for Sue Baker, our lead horn player, and Stephanie Cant has led informative workshops on Mozart and Beethoven piano concertos, followed by performances by herself and colleagues.

During one survey, the wish was expressed to play with choirs, which we have done, including Elgar's '*The Music Makers'* in

Bishop Auckland, Vaughan Williams '*Serenade to Music*' in Middlesbrough, Poulenc's *Gloria* and Verdi's *Requiem* in Newcastle. In the early days the orchestra's experience of playing with singers was honed by tackling Andy's own works, one of the finest being the *Gospel Requiem*, composed for his own Durham Scratch Choir's Voices for Hospices event.

Tracy recalls: "Another of my favourite pieces is Andy's *Gospel Requiem*. We performed it first at the Stanley Lamplight Theatre in October 2005, and it was the first time I'd ever dared to have a try at improvising. I think I felt more confident with Roderick playing loudly next to me on his saxophone! We performed it again at The Sage Gateshead the following month, conducted by David Lawrence. It was unusual for the clarinets and flutes to be sitting separately on opposite sides of the stage, and above everyone else."

In the very first newsletter, Andy wrote;

"Someone suggested that the newsletter could be used to exchange ideas on repertoire, always a huge problem. On the other hand nobody has actually made any suggestions to me yet, so I would like to make a plea on behalf of contemporary composers like myself; don't just stick to the classics, try something modern!"

Andy's compositions and arrangements (*"Sunny afternoon", La Mer*, the Beatles, etc.) have encouraged others like David Hutton and Paul Beck to try their hand at orchestration of favourite pieces which have come in handy to lighten some of our more popular concerts. Of his original compositions, Andy's *Spennyopolis* (a light hearted tribute to Spennymoor) was an early challenge, and '*Voices in Stone*' and '*The White Church*' were inspired by the majesty of Durham Cathedral. Other Cobweb members, Lizelle Kirby, ('*Shuna*' and '*Northumberland Sketchbook*') Derek Hobbs' *The Alnwick Suite*, and Stephanie Cant ('*After the Tide Turned*') have also been moved by the North East's scenery and heritage to compose for the orchestra, as has Greg Pullen, with '*Sir Bob and Sir Ted*,' referring to Sir Robert ("Bobbie") Shafto of Whitworth Hall near Spennymoor, and Sir Edward Elgar, who had links with Bishop Auckland. We are lucky enough to have some original and talented composers in our midst. We will hear from John Hawkes and Helen Pyburn in the next chapter.

We have often startled and, we hope, pleasantly surprised our audiences by breaking into a piece of film music, such as *'Pirates of the Caribbean'* or *'Jurassic Park'*. When film music was first suggested to Andy he pointed out that it was actually "much more difficult than you might think." This may be true, but these are definitely fun pieces to play and show that we are not dyed in the wool dedicatees of the classics.

Another way in which we attempt to reach out to our audiences is by involving them actively in banging, blowing or scraping some inexpensive item, among the most popular being those edible shakers known as Tubes of Smarties!

An important concomitant of repertoire is of course, programming. It is one thing to have a cupboard full of wonderful music, but there is another art in deciding which pieces to programme together to make an interesting listening experience. Andy claimed in an article in 2008: "programming for the rich and varied abilities and aspirations of Cobweb players is a bit like playing chess …. an alchemy of serendipity, strategy, tradition and opportunism guided by aesthetics and underpinned by unreasonable optimism!" He goes on to list a few examples:

Trip to Dachau: Violinist Antje Roser asked during an unguarded moment on a Tuscany trip "When are the Cobwebs coming to Germany?" Serendipity.

Wind and Brass Study Day: The wonderful Aurora Wind Quintet just happened to be in the North East giving a concert on the Friday night and was persuaded to stay on and do some tutoring the next day. Pure opportunism.

Mahler Study Day. The long term study of a major work really paid off with Franck's *D Minor Symphony*, so now we're getting to grips with Mahler. Strategy.

Annual Bishop Auckland Town Hall Concert. Tradition.

The People's Choice gave us an opportunity to vote for and then play our favourite pieces, and to pay for the privilege, thus raising some much needed cash. I think the idea was to ask outside "friends and relations" to vote, but inevitably it was the members themselves who responded most enthusiastically. We just hoped we could actually play the pieces voted for, hence the "unreasonable optimism", but in the event we chose pieces we had played and enjoyed, the most popular being - yes, the Franck *D Minor Symphony*.

A sure way to capture the delight that members experience in playing through the vast Cobwebs repertoire has been to ask them for their favourite pieces. The response has been varied but with some definite favourites. Greg, mentioned above as leader of the Spennymoor group, has a definite following who love his humorous, not to say irreverent, pieces '*Beethoven comes to Tea*' and, in Jubilee year '*Britannia waives the Rules.*' Someone said "Anything Pullen, because it is the most fun."

Overall, it is the symphonies which seem to bring the greatest thrill and satisfaction. To quote:

"Bizet's *Symphony in C* at the Sage - because it was not too hard, though the CD showed it could have been played better!"

"Bruckner's *Symphony no. 7* performed many years ago in Bowes Museum, with Chris Griffiths conducting; great performance, and a great audience - unforgettable."

Sibelius figures quite prominently, *No. 2*, "good brass section, and we did it justice) and *No. 3*, performed more recently. "Brilliant, epic proportions! It was so moving I nearly fell into that trap of getting so carried away I couldn't play."

Dvorak's *New World Symphony*: "Large orchestra, great sound!" and no. 7, "Great timpani part and great tunes."

More than one member enjoyed the Saint Saëns *Organ Symphony*, and several chose the *'Titanic'*, *Mahler's 1ˢᵗ*. One horn player recalls *Mahler 4*, "Fantastic for the horn, it covers all registers and is really challenging." And of course, Cesar *Franck's Symphony in D Minor*. "Why? Because I had never heard it before: it was totally new to me, and I loved the culmination." Another said "It makes the hairs on the back of my neck stand up."

Other favourites were Schubert's *Great C Major Symphony*, Borodin's *2ⁿᵈ* and Mendelssohn's *Italian Symphony*: "This was the first piece I played on a Study Day. I couldn't read a note the first time, but then came back 2 or 3 years later, and it made much more sense."

Others remembered pieces in the context of specific events. One person was captivated by Beethoven's *4ᵗʰ Piano Concerto* in the Sage Hall 2. "A super pianist, a magical atmosphere, everyone listening intently. We forgot about the audience as we were so wrapped up in the music."

Another event in the Sage, this time Hall 1, was Beethoven's *Coriolan Overture*, played for Clarence Adoo in preparation for a documentary on Channel 4 in which he featured, (though we didn't - very much!) Clarence always seems to challenge us to do our very best, and on this occasion, according to one player, the result was "epic."

From the Teesside group, ("a big friendly family,") "I have enjoyed playing the North East Folk Songs with the words running through my head and John's trumpet playing in *Nessun Dorma* is a definite highlight." Also remembered was William Boyce's *Symphony no. 4*. "I enjoyed playing this piece in Middlesbrough Town Hall. Afterwards I kept singing the tune and it made me feel chirpy."

Many people have fond memories of that Beethoven day; "*All* the symphonies? In one day? Such a challenge, and I didn't think it would work. But being Cobwebs, of course it did!"

Elaine (viola) "I have wonderful memories of a Bishop Auckland "Proms in the Park" where *The Lark Ascending* was played. An emotional moment was seeing the flags waving and the singing of the 1000 plus audience when I glanced to the right of my music stand."

Other memories include *"Die Fledermaus Overture*, because it is such fun!" *Night on a Bare Mountain* - the flute part is really fun to play". "Mozart's *Gran Partita*- Lovely wind group and concert," and *The Pines of Rome* played at Kielder with a hangover"- enough said.

Finally, Pauline Holbrook recalls "It must be the *"Twenty Year Kiss"* (by Andy Jackson) which we did when I first joined the orchestra. After three weeks on flute number six, I moved to percussion - very scary! There was also a neat recorder solo which really surprised Andy when I played it, on the recorder, the following week."

In an article for Making Music magazine in 2008, Andy wrote:

"Because we have a policy of never turning people away, it is important that we develop a repertoire suitable for players of vastly different musical abilities, so we are always encouraging composers to write for us, and have established a library of several hundred works…"

4. Makers and Takers: Composers, Arrangers and Others who help to Keep the Show on the Road

"Composers…"

As mentioned in the previous chapter, we are lucky to have some enthusiastic and talented composers who understand the needs and parameters of working with the Cobweb orchestra. Here, John Hawkes describes his various attempts to respond to Andy's plea for new works.

"As a composer you always expect orchestras to be falling over backwards to play your pieces and in that spirit, soon after the Alnwick weekend, I sent Andy a copy of my *Divertimento for Chamber Orchestra*. I had a letter back saying that the Cobwebs had played through it and enjoyed it and that "we're not giving concerts at the moment so I don't know when it might be programmed but not too far in the future, I hope (years rather than decades)" and indeed some 13 years later the Cobwebs did perform it in public at Morpeth!

In the summer of 1997 I started attending the Cobweb rehearsals regularly in the Annfield Plain Library and in July of that year I found myself playing in a Cobwebs concert as part of the Durham Miners' Gala. Several Sinfonia players were also present including oboist Colin Kellett, who insisted I play 1st Oboe. I hadn't got a tuner at the time and when the leader, Noel Broome, called for an 'A' for the orchestra to tune to I almost hoped the ground would open and swallow me up!

Composing for the Cobwebs always presents a considerable challenge to me because you can never be sure what instruments will be available (and of what standard) and unfortunately I regard instrumentation as one of the most important aspects of composition. One way of dealing with this is to write, say, a four part piece and let whoever turns up take an appropriate line. However, though a practical solution, to my mind this can produce a rather stodgy effect.

One of the first pieces of mine to be taken up by the Cobwebs was the *'Northumbrian Prelude'*. Originally written for a large recorder ensemble, I orchestrated it in 1996 and it was performed twice by the Cobwebs in 1999, at the Caedmon Hall, Gateshead on the 28th February (with some Northern Sinfonia 'stiffening') and on the 20th May in the Community Centre at Saltburn. I'm not at all sure how the latter gig came about (it did seem a rather unlikely venue), but I do remember being transported with the rest of the orchestra in a hired coach. Again I couldn't resist incorporating a somewhat unconventional section into the music just to liven things up a bit, where the conductor stops conducting and all the players set off at their own speed.

2006 saw a collaboration between Caedmon Folk and the Cobwebs and I was asked (along with Derek Hobbs and Andy Jackson) if I would like to compose a piece involving both groups for a concert in Hall 2 of the Sage on Sunday 8th October. The result was *'Silver and Gold'* which uses thematic material from the tunes *'Silver Street Lasses'* and *'If I had Gold'*. My treatment of folk material tends to be rather un-reverential, I'm afraid, and I battered the tunes about! The piece was intended to have a rather 'primitive' even brutal feel to it, and involved the wind players banging stones together from time to time (Cobwebs meets the *Rite of Spring*??). The folk people were rather baffled by it I fear!

Some four years later, on the 21st March 2010 my *Divertimento* was finally performed by the Cobwebs at a concert in Morpeth. (By a quirk of fate the same piece was performed on the very same day by the Warwick Youth Orchestra: you wait ages for a bus and then...) In the same concert Alice Jones performed the Elgar *Cello Concerto*, and I was bowled over by the quality of her playing. On the spur of the moment and rather cheekily I asked if I could write a piece for her. Fortunately she agreed and the result was the *Concertino for Cello and Orchestra*. This time I decided to stick with a more conventional approach to musical notation! Alice played the piece at the Sedbergh residential weekend in 2011 and again in Appleby on 22nd October the same year. She also recorded the piece in May 2012 with a (mainly) Cobweb ensemble.

As well as composing opportunities, the Cobwebs have provided several interesting conducting opportunities (and not just of my own pieces). I particularly remember an occasion in 1997 in Bishop Auckland when 5 conductors tackled Beethoven's *5th Symphony*. The first 3 movements had just one conductor each but in the finale I had to take over from David Plews half way through. I wonder if anyone noticed!

Of course my most constant connection with the Cobwebs has been through playing the oboe, and what a fantastic range of playing opportunities there have been! Highlights for me have included Sibelius's *2nd Symphony*, Carl Orff's *Carmina Burana*, several symphonies of Mahler not to mention all of Beethoven's symphonies in one day. And what of the future? Well, having purchased the score, there is now the very real possibility of the Cobwebs meeting the *Rite of Spring*."

And indeed it has been done, with great enthusiasm and a lot of noise!

Another of our members who discovered a talent for composing is the late Helen Pyburn. She wrote the following in the programme notes to the *Horn Concerto* she wrote for Sue Baker:

"I wrote the *Horn Concerto* for Sue in 2010, at her suggestion, at a time when she knew I needed to be occupied by a fruitful project to fill my time and distract me from my everyday problems and worries. In the second movement particularly, the concerto is based on two very different pieces of well-known popular music, Lou Reed's '*It's such a perfect day*' and Monty Python's '*Always look on the bright side of life.*' The first movement was written in 5/4 time with the intention of being a slight tongue-in-cheek challenge for the orchestra, a challenge which they took on admirably. I have no formal training in composition beyond O-level Music, but thoroughly enjoy writing for the Cobweb Orchestra, whose members are incredibly tolerant of my offerings!"

The orchestra has also been delighted to perform several other works by Helen, including *Alchemy and Quicksilver, Little Miss Muffet, Under the Influence*, and *A Parody of Time*, conceived at her husband's bedside in hospital and inspired by the noise of monitors and other equipment which punctuated the silence of the ward. On Tuesday 4th June 2013, around fifty members of the Cobweb orchestra played this and a selection of other works composed or arranged by Helen, after her funeral in St. Peter's Church, Bywell, Northumberland.

"and Arrangers"

Even people who play in orchestras are not always aware of what instruments are required to play particular works. For instance, (Andy wrote) Mozart and Haydn wrote 145 symphonies between them but less than twenty of them have parts for clarinets and none of them include trombones. Because we want to encourage EVERYONE to play orchestral music, we try whenever possible to create parts which allow all to participate.

Most baroque orchestral music is for string orchestra with continuo, with an occasional smattering of woodwind and brass. To play this repertoire as a whole orchestra requires extensive re-writing by our Composers and Arrangers group, who have provided a massive amount of baroque music which can now be played by everyone.

At the other end of the spectrum, and the historical time line, there may be music which includes saxophones or an electric bass, but no strings. So the question is; do we play this music in its original form in which case some people are excluded, or do we do our best to give everyone the chance to participate? To some extent the smaller specialist groups (see Ch. 2) have helped out here, but there is still the occasion when a saxophone player comes to an full evening session, and saxophone parts are usually found to be available in any set of our music that has been "Cobwebbed".

David Hutton gives his perspective on the arranger's task:

"Andy is familiar with the demands of groups whose members are not always able to attend every week and which could be joined by unexpected others (like an accordion player, yes, it did happen) or in amazing combinations or numbers (at our tenth birthday celebrations at Hexham we had 14 clarinets), so he has already been writing flexible arrangements to suit a core of just a few essential players (3 basic parts), and expandable to include any player who could join in. And while many of our arrangements aspire to this approach we, as players, are also encouraged to be flexible. After all, those many flautists could just as well play from a violin part, and clarinettists could even read from a viola part - with a bit of practice."

This brings us nicely to the knotty problem of transposing. Lizelle Kirby wrote this piece for a newsletter.

"You just stick it in the scanner and press a button, don't you? Oh, if only! For those of us who regularly tackle this issue, we could pool our experiences and write an entire book! I hope what follows offers a brief glimpse of some of the processes involved.

Scenario 1. Yes, we have no violas! So, transpose the parts for clarinets. They do have a similar range, but it is frustrating when you just need that one note lower than the violas have access to. Leaping up an octave is going to spoil that lovely melody. (For the sceptics among you, yes, the violas do sometimes get a good tune!) Maybe we should put the whole section, or phrase, up an octave so it doesn't sound so angular. And how can we expect clarinets to play pizzicato, or tremolo? Decisions, decisions….

Scenario 2. We have saxophones! Now, what did Bach write for the saxophone? Well, there are some horn parts, let's transpose them. The horn is an amazing instrument with an incredible range. The saxophone is also amazing. I have to say that as mine sits on its stand next to my desk. But the sax cannot match the range of the horn. It also has a completely different timbre and cannot equal the dynamics. In other words, a sax is *not* a horn. Horns frequently play a wonderful role in providing rich, warm chordal textures that involve notes too low for the sax. If we shift these notes an octave higher we are not really just transposing any more, we are *arranging*. It will not sit within the texture of the orchestra in the same way, and can dramatically change the effect. One solution would be to leave it at written pitch just transposing the key and leaving the players or conductor to decide how to treat it, for example, if someone else has that part, say a real-genuine-article horn, then leave it to them ... but then your sax player will think you have forgotten them, or just don't know/understand the range of their instrument. We can always clutter up the transposed part with written information of the if/but/maybe type, but this can take a considerable amount of time and is not easy to read at a glance when playing at sight (as we so often are).

Scenario 3. "I've just bought a snufflephone (shall we say!) Can I come and play it at Cobwebs?" Our response is always "Of course you can!" I did once have a player come up to me and say "Well, it isn't very idiomatic writing for a snufflephone" I'm afraid that if Handel didn't write for the snufflephone then a transposition is *never* going to be idiomatic writing for it.

All this aside there are the technicalities of getting the music from one format to another. If you start off with a beautifully clear piece of music, size A4, nothing too rhythmically complex, then you're onto a winner and can get to that waiting bottle of Merlot all the quicker. But more often than not we have ancient copies that won't fit on the scanner, and are smudged, damaged and difficult for *us* to read, let alone our software. It can often take two hours to get the average part - one movement only - from the original to a transposed part, and sometimes considerably longer. So next time your transposed copy isn't quite up to scratch, spare a thought for the Cobwebber who gave up his/her time to bring more music to your stand. It is never quite straightforward, and it certainly isn't as simple as pressing a button!"

An article by Helen Pyburn in the Spring 2012 newsletter demonstrates the studious and detailed nature of some of their training sessions.

"On Saturday 19th November we had an excellent three hour session led by composer and Morpeth group leader, Lizelle Kirby. We met in the wonderful music room of Andrew Cottrell's house, with the use of laptop, speakers and projection screen if necessary. After a brief introduction, Lizelle put the group through their paces, with such delights as the Circle of Fifths, rhythmic augmentation and diminution, retrograde rhythm and pitch, and such compositional devices as fragmentation, repetition and pitch alteration, inversion and finally, use of octatonic scales. She was able to demonstrate her use of the octatonic scale which was based on three diminished 7th chords. She used this scale as the basis of her wind quintet '*Quiddity*.'"

The Musicologist's Tale

Brian Tanner, who plays double bass with the Consett group, is lucky enough to own a History of Music by Emil Naumann written in the 1880s, and therefore something of a period piece in itself. (Naumann discusses the potential of Johannes Brahms, in a chapter headed "The Present" in the same guarded terms that we use when considering the works of contemporary composers today.) In a chapter on "Modern English Music" he writes of one Philip Cipriani Hambly Potter, known as "Little Chip" because he was rather short in stature, who lived from 1792 to 1871. He was Professor of Pianoforte at the Royal Academy of Music from 1822 till 1859, composed nine symphonies and a vast amount of piano music. Naumann also quotes from a letter from Beethoven, which said:

"Potter has visited me several times. He seems to be a good man, and has talent for composition."

Feeling that if he was good enough for Beethoven he was good enough for Cobwebs, Brian went along to the British Library and found the parts of a *Duo Concertant for Violin, Piano and Orchestra*, of which he duly obtained copies, it being well out of copyright. Thus was the Potter Project born. Pauline Holbrook undertook an initial preparation of the parts, in itself no small task, and a first play through took place in October 2001 at Durham School under the baton of the Head of Music there, Roger Muttitt. This was almost certainly the first performance for 170 years. A large orchestra assembled for this event and it was decided that it was worth another try after some cutting and re-arranging to make it "more interesting for wind players." After a second run in Durham, the "new, improved version" was eventually given a major outing at the Stanwix Arts Theatre in Carlisle in July 2002, with Rachael Davis on the violin and Stephanie Cant at the piano. It was agreed to have been worth the trouble of researching, processing, re-orchestrating and rehearsing, "a charmingly idiosyncratic work which fits into the Cobweb repertoire perfectly." It was also felt that Potter may well have approved, since he was apparently adept at "adapting" the concertos of Mozart and Beethoven to the practice needs of his pupils.

The performance was recorded for a CD, and it was hoped that the work "could be taken up by other adventurous orchestras." It was great to hear that the Potter *Concertant* was revived again in 2013 at the Sedbergh residential.

Another good friend of the orchestra has been performer, composer and general all-round supporter, Stephanie Cant. Here Stephanie reflects on her time and contribution to Cobwebs.

"I came to live in Durham City in the autumn of 1998, having previously lived and worked as a composer, pianist and teacher on the Sussex coast near Brighton. The Cobweb Orchestra came into my life in stages. Quite early on, another musician with whom I had become briefly acquainted told me that I really should go and see Andy Jackson. So I did. We met at his (then) office at the DLI Museum and Art Gallery, and we talked about my possibly composing or arranging for the orchestra, which at that moment was a smallish group of players meeting in Annfield Plain Library on a Thursday night.

After listening to a tape of a piece of mine which I had thought might be adaptable, Andy phoned to invite me to arrange it for the orchestra. I said it would be good to come and listen to them play first. Andy said:' Didn't I play an orchestral instrument?' I should come to play – nobody just *listened*. Should I come 'empty handed' - some instrument or other way of joining in would be found. At that point I was very grateful that I did have a cello, and, I was in fact, unbeknownst to me, a true Cobweb, as I am sure I had to dust the cello down before I brought it along.

I arrived at the due moment - along with 5 other cellists. Yet the total number of players was barely 20, and 4 of the others were flutes! A horn, a bassoon, a double bass, a couple of violins, 2 violas and 2 clarinets made up the rest. How to write for this?

Andy advised to think in terms of three voices – top middle and bottom. That way, 'adaptable instruments' like a horn or clarinet could be assigned variously depending on who else was there. (First lesson.)

My *Suite for Orchestra*, fashioned from a piece for three recorders, thus came into being. I had taken Andy's advice literally, and when the moment came, gave out the parts as required. During the tea break Jeremy the horn player came up to me, and gently but firmly explained that the horn was not a recorder and that there were far too many notes and too little time to take the breaths required, even if a 'stab' were to be made at what I had actually written, which actually I couldn't really expect. Andy I think was playing the trumpet, which probably had the same problems, though he was less forthright. (He didn't need to be – Jeremy had said it.)

I went away and re-wrote the score with the 'difficult' instruments no longer participating in everything, but coming and going in a way that actually proved to be an enhancement of the orchestration. The piece entered the Cobweb repertoire and thus began to be performed all over the place (the repertoire at that point was not huge and nothing was 'wasted') from Durham City, to Hexham, and from Hebburn to an open air event in a walled garden on a night in June which might have been warm but was actually extremely cold and involved the assembled audience gradually disappearing under the rugs they had brought to sit on, whilst the orchestral players systematically froze, but played on. (Second lesson.)

Despite these early hiccups I found myself rather enjoying the challenge of writing for such an enthusiastic and supportive bunch of players and I determined to experiment with arranging the music of other composers. Gabrieli and Handel sprang to mind and I arranged a couple of Canzonas by the former, and a Prelude by the latter. Meanwhile I was also enjoying playing the cello in an orchestra again and as a result of my informal participation, my next orchestration challenge came along in an unexpected guise; the opportunity to play a Mozart concerto for a study day for Cobwebs at the Sinfonia centre on the Steinway D housed there. What a treat I thought – which it was.

But it was also a learning curve as four oboes signed up (K 488 does not have even one oboe part) and also a trombone. How do I arrange parts for them that would be fun for the players, but not usurp the legitimate parts for other players that Mozart had written? This is possibly the most important skill which a Cobweb composer can learn. And, though I didn't know this in this way at that time, in doing that arrangement in respect of a work which I had known and played since I was

15, I was able to lay a most important foundation stone for all my subsequent writing for the orchestra. (Third lesson).

Following on from this, I received a commission from the Orchestra (funded by Wear Valley District Council) to compose a piece for an 'Elgar Day' at Bishop Auckland Town Hall. I and three other composers were asked to write something which 'bounced off' a piece by Elgar which we would then conduct 'against' our own piece. I chose Elgar's *Romance for Bassoon and Orchestra*, and thus composed *Italian Serenade,* the first movement of which was written in Italy, near Alassio where Elgar also had gone in the winter sometimes.

I had also taken on board many aspects of writing for a flexible group and, with the increasing number of players, my basic three voice structure gave way to a four voice structure. Again, as in the three part writing, some loud, difficult to play, or otherwise problematic instruments had parts tailored for their needs, but still based on those four parts.

By the time that performance came along, the orchestra had grown more 'tentacles' and nearly 60 players came along to perform these pieces. I probably need not have gone to such lengths to write parts that were adaptable depending on which players turned up. They all had! (Fourth lesson). However, the adaptability did prove useful at a later stage, when the piece travelled to Tuscany with the orchestra on two separate occasions.

However, the strictures of orchestration with which I had become used to working to ensure the survival of any piece regardless of who turned up had gradually become semi-internalised and in fact formed a second 'plank' in the armoury I was building up with regard to composing and arranging for the orchestra – the first plank being the skill (learnt on the Mozart) of providing parts which enabled players to join in, even if the piece as originally conceived would not have involved them.

For the tenth anniversary of the orchestra, I arranged a set of variations on *La Folia*, which was performed at the birthday party, and later in a concert at the Sage, Gateshead, before, like *Italian*

Serenade, taking its place in the baggage going to Tuscany. At the same time, I was composing a choral and orchestral work, *You can shed tears,* in memory of a dear Cobweb friend Anne Wilder, one of the viola players on that very first night I had come to the orchestra in 1999. She had had also sung in Durham Choral Society, who were to perform the work in Durham Cathedral in May 2006. However I had Cobwebs in mind too as I wrote, and may yet discover a purely orchestral version for the orchestra in the long run from various related orchestral sketches which were not included in the final choral work. The Cobweb Orchestra did play through the choral piece at one of the Thursday evening rehearsals. Further, what I had written for the named group of instruments associated with the Choral Society's orchestra survived a performance by the ad hoc Cobweb orchestra present at the rehearsal.

It was at that point, I realised that my apprenticeship had ended. I could now compose 'intuitively' for orchestral forces in a way that made sense to the players and was robust enough to work, even if not every instrument which should be there was there. In addition, I now realise that I had also learned ways of writing music which was enjoyable and fun to play, a quality not always present in contemporary scores, which has also been appreciated by the professional performers in various solo/chamber combinations for whom I also write.

My works for the orchestra have continued with *After the Tide Turned* (2009), enjoyed by a number of the weekly groups and programmed in Darlington and York, with the second movement, '*Machines,*' also featuring at the concert for the Queen at the opening of the Wild Waters on Teesside in a form for wind and brass in July 2012. Most recently my new '*Lament*' for horn and orchestra was given a workout at the Sedbergh Easter Residential in 2013.

Unfortunately I have now departed from the North East and am back in Sussex from whence I came. However I will continue to cherish the skills I have built during my sojourn in the North and I will not forget my friends in the Cobweb Orchestra. I will be back!"

The Librarian's Tale

Having the music there on the stands at the beginning of a rehearsal is something which can easily be taken for granted, until something goes wrong: a transposed clarinet part not provided, a transcribed part for nose flute not available. (Well, not quite, but that sort of thing!) As Liz wrote in a newsletter:

"Everything the library does is behind the scenes, and the better it is done, the more behind the scenes it appears (or disappears) to be."

It used to be a job for one - now there is a Librarian for each group and the challenge of where to keep the music continues. This is one of the main challenges of the music library, -where to keep the ever growing collection. The other is that of keeping track of the music ...

These are the memories of Lee, Liz and Ruth of how the library has grown - and grown - over the years.

Lee recalls the early days and says that she never had to carry the music as there was always someone on hand to help out. Ruth, who has a bad back, (Why do I DO this job??) supports this. "Always ensure there is a strong and willing helper to hand!" A supply of small wheeled carts, designed originally for craft work, now supplement the variety of bags, from supermarket 'bags for life' to the works of art created by Lee, Pauline *et al*.

Liz took over the library after the first Tuscany trip, when it was contained in four Curver baskets, and later in one filing cabinet. It gradually grew to fill four or five filing cabinets and now occupies many feet of shelving. There are over 300 sets of music of all sorts, shapes, sizes and descriptions;

symphonies, songs, concertos, gifts, commissions, original compositions and arrangements. Sets of music are now supplemented by transpositions and arrangements by Andy or Helen, Derek or Lizelle, plus extra parts for our sometimes very peculiar shaped orchestra, as described by Stephanie and Lizelle.

The venue for the collection proved a problem, and it has travelled over the years from Andy and Sue's landing cupboard, to the basement of the Sage, thence via a freezing cold roof space on the Stockton campus of Durham University, and a cupboard in the CAB offices in Bishop Auckland to Liz's house.

We now ask members to download their own parts for study if possible, so that we don't have to lend out hired copies. Previously the librarian used to send out parts on request, with dire warnings as to the consequences if they did not re-appear, and then had to ensure that they were indeed returned in time to be checked and sent back to the library. Those small individual parts could so easily get lost on top of the piano, or slipped into some other music, down the side of the sofa …

Liz again: " The library is in constant use, with music going in and out all the time, for the regular groups, study days, concerts, and occasionally to groups who are not part of Cobwebs. Along with this constant use goes constant sorting, counting and filing, checking, repairing and labelling …"

It seems an endless task and each new person coming to the job tries, innocently, a new system or cunning plan to make the task easier or more fool-proof. Unfortunately, grim reality soon kicks in.

One of the nicer aspects are the Library days at Liz's house, when a modicum of checking is carried out by volunteers, if not too distracted by other delights such as tea, cake, chat, cake, playing – and more cake!

The Archivist

The archives, along with the newsletters and individual people's memories, have provided the majority of the material for this book, and so we have reason to be grateful to anyone who takes on this behind-the-scenes but very useful role. Chrissie Macgregor has recently taken over from Helen Pyburn as Keeper of the Cobweb Archives and wrote a piece about them, and about her predecessor, for the newsletter. Here is an excerpt.

"It is fascinating to see the changing face of the orchestra, as well as the changing faces of Cobwebbers, since 1995, not least from the perspective of graphic design. There were long years of faltering from one Cobweb-themed logo to another until the Cobwebs look was created in 2008 with the inspired and versatile logo designed by viola player Joan Murray.

The Archive itself reflects something of the archivist, and in Helen's case you get a strong sense of her dedication and devotion to Cobwebs. In addition to the everyday filing, there are tickets from the many Sage study days she attended as well as detailed records of foreign residentials, including pieces of music she composed following trips to Dachau and Tuscany. To have kept up the archive so conscientiously despite serious illness is quite something. Helen, you were amazing."

5. Special Events

In a sense every Cobweb event is special. Many are in unusual venues, both indoors and out, many include new works, often composed specially for us, or concertos where we are privileged to accompany fine soloists. Some have been for particular occasions. Sometimes we target families with young children, or join in local celebrations at the Sage Gateshead or at 'Proms in the Park' at Bishop Auckland.

The concert in Benfieldside in 1996 was special because it was the first, and the Mahler Challenge in January 1997 was special because it was a large and daring undertaking, including professional colleagues and fellow musicians from other groups. Both of these were of course at the very beginning of Cobwebs' life cycle. What follows is just a selection of events which have stood out from the rest over the years for various reasons.

Art, Music and Theatre combine at the Bowes Museum

Early members of Cobwebs recall with delight an event held in the Bowes Museum, Barnard Castle in 1997 when they played at the opening of an 'Art of the Theatre' exhibition at which the guest speaker was actress, Jane Lapotaire. There was only one player per part as it was the first day of the summer holidays, but they managed a high standard and members of the 200-strong audience were surprised that "an amateur group could play so well." Those who were not there can only imagine the thrill of playing against the backdrop of the Canaletto, the El Greco and other great paintings in the galleries of that sumptuous and amazing, French chateau-style building built by John and Josephine Bowes in the nineteenth century.

Spennyopolis.

'Spennyopolis: Symphony for a City' arose out of an on-going collaboration between Andy Jackson and artist Anton Hecht and was the first of several joint ventures for Cobwebs. It was first performed in Bowes Museum, Barnard Castle in May 1997. Andy wrote the music to accompany a photographic

and video installation by Anton celebrating the life of a simple, unremarkable County Durham town. Andy described Anton's work as "using high art to explore low life."

Bridie Jackson, who sang on the CD version, wrote on the cover:

"A piece of music dedicated to the small town of Spennymoor in County Durham. "Why?" the listener might ask, but is it not just as valid a question to ask "Why not?" Gershwin wrote about America, Respighi of Rome, and now Andy Jackson writes of the glories to be beheld in Spennymoor in this four minute long symphony - a "symphony for a city".

Spennyopolis, although definitely to be taken with tongue in cheek, nevertheless celebrates the normalities of a real place, not put there to impress or even particularly to please people: it has no pretences as to what it is, no pretty floral arrangements or garish gift shops. It is a place where people live, die, work and play bingo!

I sang *Spennyopolis* for the first time in Spennymoor itself, in the bandstand on a particularly cold September morning. We were a collection of nervous amateur musicians, gathered together in a disorganised group, stamping our feet and drinking coffee from thermos flasks in an attempt to keep warm, and although certainly noticed by the people of Spennymoor that day, we did not receive quite the enthusiastic reception we had hoped for. It has since been performed many times and is now an established and popular part of the Cobwebs repertoire."

Later, further rather crazy projects were undertaken with Anton, including one memorable day when musicians gathered around the Angel of the North, as Tracy remembers:

"Anton's '*Morphing Music*' in October 2005 featured many musicians in different locations in Gateshead. Ten of us from Cobwebs were filmed at the Angel of the North. We weren't told we would be wearing boiler suits. 'One size fits all' isn't true- I was compared to a Teletubby! We had to memorise a few bars of music then walk along playing and stop. Frank (Robson) had to be wheeled along on a trolley with his cello and he actually fell off!"

COBWEBS GO UNDERCOVER: FLASH MOB 'BOLERO' by Chrissie Macgregor

On 13 February 2010 a group of players from the Cobweb Orchestra joined Andy Jackson for a film project he was doing with his long-time collaborator, the film-maker Anton Hecht. The idea was to film a flash mob rendition of Ravel's *Bolero* in Eldon Square Bus Station.

The resulting film, *Undercover Orchestra 'Bolero' classical flash mob 'kinda'*, has now received over half a million views on You Tube (508,253 as I write, almost 10,000 in the last fortnight) – surely our biggest audience to date. It was for this film that the Cobweb Orchestra won the Voluntary Arts England Epic Award for Innovation, which Andy Jackson and Trustee Elizabeth Beer received on behalf of the orchestra at the House of Lords on 31 January 2011. All in all, this project turned out to be something a good deal bigger than any of us involved had anticipated.

The idea behind *Undercover Orchestra* was to make classical music more accessible by performing it in an unusual place. The scenario: 'Players will appear to be travellers waiting for buses, but, once they hear the familiar rhythm of Ravel's Bolero tapped out on a briefcase, will be unable to resist the urge to take an instrument out of their clothing/rucksack/briefcase and join in. Four minutes later, they will be part of an orchestra blasting out the concluding bars of this overplayed but glorious score.'

Andy arranged a four-minute version of '*Bolero*' especially for the film. It contains every note of the original, but he subjected it to a 'time and efficiency review'. It was performed by Cobwebs players as they walked through the bus station, surrounded by Eldon Square shoppers and people waiting for buses.

The players had parts written especially for them and were sent the music ten days before the filming was due to take place. Just ten days for people to memorise their parts or devise a method of reading their music surreptitiously while on the move. An hour's rehearsal on the day ended with a back-up recording, just in case of disaster during the performance. The film itself was shot in one take, starting without announcement at 11.30 am on the dot, catching some of us by surprise. Our playing was accompanied by the clicking of press photographers' cameras and the general hubbub of a busy bus station on a Saturday morning.

In retrospect it was terrifying, for me at any rate, especially as the You Tube hits started to clock up (30,000 in the first week alone) but at the time we all seemed to be enjoying ourselves too much to panic. Afterwards it was a comfort to know that at least nobody had tripped or forgotten their notes, especially as some of us were playing from memory for the first time.

As often seems to happen, where the Cobweb Orchestra goes, others eventually follow. In this case, professional symphony orchestra the Copenhagen Philharmonic did a similar flash mob '*Bolero*' on Copenhagen Central Station just over a year after ours. They performed their version standing still, with their music on stands and their conductor in front of them throughout. It makes us look rather brave (or possibly foolhardy) in comparison.

The '*Bolero*' film seems to sum up much of what Cobwebs is about – enthusiasm, enjoyment and new musical experiences, supported by Andy's special blend of relaxed good humour, precision with regard to musical matters, patience with his players and ability to encourage them to do more than they could have imagined possible."

Tracy reveals the 'cunning plan' devised for those not quite brave enough to rely on their memory:

"Taking part in the '*Undercover Orchestra*' in the Eldon Square bus station was really funny. My clarinet was hidden in my rucksack and my music for Bolero was taped onto Julie's back. I had to listen hard for the opening to know when to start, and I'll never forget the expression on the faces of two ladies sitting opposite when I started to play. I then had to keep up with Julie moving swiftly through the bus station, trying to avoid passengers on the way."

Music and Silence

In June 1998, a group of Cobwebbers vividly remembers one Saturday morning when they toured round 3 local libraries in a minibus with cellist Jeanette Mountain, playing, as Andy put it, the overture in Newton Hall, intermezzo in Consett and the finale in Bishop Auckland. The strap line on the promotional poster was "See it, hear it, live it, because words can't describe it!" The concept of 'Shhh!' in the library was obviously shelved on this occasion.

Then in July of 2000, Andy organised an event in Bishop Auckland library called "Playing with Silence." Andy described it as an installation, where the exhibits were the musicians. The evening comprised playing snatches of music, improvising on snippets of music posted up around the room, and allowing for long periods of silence, culminating in a performance of music gradually drawn together from outline instructions. This was the second such event conceived and directed by Andy. The first was in Kendal, Cumbria, and was entitled "Unbearable Beauty surrounded by Silence", inspired by the form of a Quaker Meeting, so that musicians were encouraged to play whenever they felt moved to do so. The Bishop Auckland event had a slightly different focus, and was much more structured, encouraging the contemplation of the role of silence in music and "why we feel less inclined to be quiet when requested than we used to." The first event evoked such comments as "My ears are twice as large" and "Going to a concert will never be the same." At the time of writing this memoir, the role of silence in music is again a topic being considered by musicians and musicologists, another example of Andy and Cobwebs having been ahead of the game by a good 12 years.

Music in a Public Place

In March 2000 Cobwebs played for late-night shoppers in Eldon Garden Shopping Centre, Newcastle, as part of National Orchestra Week. More than usually exact instructions were given about what to bring, including "a folding chair and spares of everything in case people turn up who have not received this letter." (This was in the days before extensive use of e-mails, remember!) Refreshments were not a problem, however, as "we are playing in an area in front of the café."

In November of the same year they returned to Eldon Square to play for evening shoppers in Marks and Spencer's on the night the Christmas lights were turned on. This was by way of a "thank-you" to M&S who were major financial supporters of the orchestra at the time.

"Sell-By"

"Andy Jackson's third opera, but the first to carry a bar-code."

This community arts venture to create an opera "from scratch" was born of Andy's vision coupled with the enthusiasm of his Durham WEA Singing from Scratch group, which in honour of the work became the Durham People's Opera Group, or DPOG.

Michael Standen, sometime District Secretary of the Workers' Educational Association, and long-time tutor, writer and poet, facilitated the writing of a libretto in the Autumn of 1998 through a course called 'Let's Write an Opera', following a series of Day Schools, working with a group of creative writers drawn largely from the choir .As it said on the advertising poster: "a script starts with an idea, which comes from a pioneering writing group whose challenge is to find ideas, theme, plot, characters - the crucial development stage of the People's Opera." Could this spontaneous ("home grown but not homespun") and organic process work?

Andy led a similar group in composing and preparing the work for performance on a course called "Now Let's write the Music" during which it was recorded that "periods of serious thought were often punctuated by moments of hilarity." Well within the Cobwebs tradition then.

Together with the Cobweb Orchestra the work saw the light of day first at the Lamplight Theatre in Stanley on 5th and 6th July 2001, when a group of rather shell-shocked performers stepped tentatively into the limelight, and then on Sunday 8th they took to the stage of the Linbury Studio Theatre at the Royal Opera House. Twenty-five members of Cobwebs and three instrumentalists from the Royal Opera House provided orchestral support, all under the baton of Alan Fearon of Northern Sinfonia, and the whole production was sponsored by Durham City Arts, Derwentside District Council, the Millennium Festival and Northern Arts - a truly collaborative enterprise, and one which stretched actors and singers alike to new experiences beyond their wildest dreams.

The story takes place in a genetic engineering plant, and revolves around those "stored-uns" kept frozen and ultimately disposed of by sending them "to the wheelie-bins!" when their "sell-by dates" have expired, and the compassion of Angel who tries to dodge the system and save the condemned. Although not really resolved, the story with its hints of George Orwell, is an imaginative if not downright scary one, giving great scope for a dramatic musical arrangement which Andy approached with relish and the orchestra with gusto!

Lee Fairlie, who chaired DPOG at the time, as well as being a Cobweb member, reflects on the event.

"As I look over the list of many participants in this venture over a decade ago, I am reminded of the immense enjoyment, hard work and sheer terror we shared. Time has taken some of the participants away, but many are still active Cobweb and Scratch Choir members. Thanks, Andy."

Handel on the Wear June 2002

Pauline Holbrook wrote: "In mid-June, after a week of rain, we all turned up unbelievably on a fine day to play Handel's *Water Music* beside and ON the River Wear at Sunderland. The sun shone, so we and the audience kept dry and although it was too windy to perform on the roof of the Glass Centre as planned, we were able to perform outside on the University Piazza where the awning had been erected to protect us and our music from the gentle summer zephyrs (North-East style!)

While the predicted overwhelming numbers of young children didn't turn up, we had a solid recorder section and several able youngsters scattered through each section of the orchestra. After several hours of rehearsal in various groups, we all came together for a run through before the final performance.

The audience was enthusiastic but the greatest admiration was reserved for the Quintessentials, who, lashed to the deck of a small boat (a veteran of Dunkirk), played the second suite of the *Water Music* as they glided down the river.

Once again we had an event which suited both experienced players and the less able, and gave an introduction to orchestral playing to many children. I hope they enjoyed the experience as much as we did - and it was really nice to have the support of a talented young percussionist on the back row."

The Gospel Requiem

This was another enterprise in association with Andy's "Scratch" Choir. Here he describes the background to the composition of the *Gospel Requiem*.

"After our "Voices for Hospices" charity performance of *Carmina Burana* in 2003, I started to look round for a choral work which was similarly accessible to all: singers who may not be experienced sight-readers, and players of all instruments who like to be involved throughout a performance, which ruled out everything before Mozart because early composers only used half the instruments of the modern orchestra, and almost everything after Mozart because it was too difficult.

The solution was to create a new work based on existing gospel songs, some well-known, some obscure and some compiled from a variety of sources. The same approach was to be applied to the music too, but here some of the music would be my own, written using the same idiom. The resulting *Gospel Requiem* was to have something for everyone: great tunes to sing for mainly melody people, challenging harmonies for part singers and plenty of involvement for instrumentalists."

Over one hundred singers and players gave the first performance at the Lamplight Theatre in Stanley on Saturday 8th October 2005. Word quickly got round that it was a worthwhile piece to perform, and by the time of the second airing in Hall 1 of The Sage Gateshead in November conductor David Lawrence was confronted by an orchestra and choir of over two hundred. About half of these made it back to The Sage Gateshead in early January 2006 to record this CD.

'*A Gospel Requiem*' presents some thoughts about death from a humanist point of view. It roughly follows the format of the traditional Requiem Mass with nine sections mapping out an emotional and philosophical journey which explores the nature of mortality.

Most of the pieces are designed so that male and female voices can sing the melody if they do not want to tackle the harmony and also to enable the audience to join in with some of the better-known numbers such as '*Down by the Riverside*' or '*This Little Light of Mine*', or indeed any of the numbers if they were given the words and possibly the melody-lines in the programme.

One notable feature of the score is the use of clarinet and flute choirs, each of which "has a precise function: the clarinets are employed as a substitute for the choral sound when words are no longer necessary, whereas the flutes explore an ethereal sound world which is largely unobtainable by the human voice."

The large orchestral resources required for this piece mean that it can only be performed in large venues in this current form, so Andy created a more "portable" version accompanied by a smaller band and this new arrangement received the first of several performances in July 2006.

Heaven Beneath Our Feet

'Heaven Beneath Our Feet' was also written by Andy for a Voices for Hospices event. Back in the mid-nineties along with a fellow gardener, Jem Warr, he had written a work called 'The Allotmenteers' which he describes as "a musical play about urban regeneration, love and vegetables." This work had toured widely and played to audiences of allotment gardeners as well as the "usual crowd" at arts centres and theatres. One scene featured the ghost of Gerrard Winstanley, the 17th century Civil War pamphleteer and chronicler of the political movement known as the Diggers. Winstanley's direct, powerful and beautiful language expresses the desire of the "poor and dispossessed of the land" to take control of their own destiny. His critique of how the commercial interests of his day perverted the use of the land seemed as relevant in the early 21st century as in 1649 when the Diggers set up their short-lived farming commune on waste land near Weybridge. So on the 450th anniversary of the founding of the movement, Andy wrote 'Heaven Beneath Our Feet: a communal song-cycle for voices and instruments' using Winstanley's words, and tunes from John Playford's 1651 publication, 'The English Dancing Master.'

This composition was first performed by the Scratch Choir and Cobweb Orchestra in Elvet Methodist Church, Durham in 2009, and like the Gospel Requiem before it, was a moving and memorable event. It has received many subsequent outings, (including being used to accompany a history lecture to celebrate the WEA's centenary in the North-East). In September 2013, it was performed at the Diggers' Festival in Wigan, Winstanley's home town.

Proms in the Park

An event which has become a fixture in the Cobwebs' diary is the annual summer 'Proms in the Park' concert. This began at the invitation of Wear Valley District council and was often held in the beautiful grounds of Auckland Castle, Bishop Auckland. More recently the uncertain future of the Castle has meant we have worked out of Bishop Auckland College. But also we have acquired more invitations to perform at such events, and in 2013 we also performed at Penrith and Langdon Beck, both in Cumbria, in addition to Ravenstonedale. Each year has seen a slight variation or added attraction to our programme, which, like the London Last Night of the Proms has scope for music from our own repertoire in the first half, and then the traditional rousing patriotic tunes, communal singing and fireworks in the second half. We have been privileged to welcome some brilliant soloists, including Boriana Nakeva and Min-Jin Kim, but perhaps the most eminent was Catherine Bott, a professional and internationally renowned soprano, and well-known (to Radio 3 listeners) presenter of the Early Music Show. She delighted us all with her enthusiasm and good humour, and was amused to be conducted by one of our number, Brian Tanner, in the Alleluia from Mozart's 'Exultate Jubilate'. Brian had won the right to conduct the orchestra in a raffle. Andy was a little taken aback when Brian claimed his dues for this particular occasion, but finally said "Oh, all right then." Catherine's comment was "I've never been won in a raffle before!" and gamely agreed to the deal. She was particularly complimentary about the orchestra's sensitive skills as accompanists. So, what happens elsewhere? We were left pondering.

Of course like any outdoor fixture in England in the summer, this one has seen us squelching through mud in high heels, coping with high winds with the help of our trusty clothes pegs, and even worrying about the sun melting the varnish on our cellos. Thank goodness for a new acquisition, made possible with support from our fund-raising group, Cobfriends, our very own marquee.

Middlesbrough at Easter: the Big Play.

Since 2011, a new tradition is becoming established in Cobwebs, that of spending Easter Monday in Middlesbrough Town Hall at a 'Big Play'. Andy, having hatched the idea of a get-together of all the Cobwebs groups, contacted Middlesbrough Town Hall (a 'big space for a big play')-enquiring about hiring the hall for a day in the Easter break. In the event, only Bank Holiday Monday was available. We knew that the building was ideal for such a venture, having used it for several choral and orchestral performances, including Beethoven's 9th symphony in 2010. So, unlikely as it seemed, Andy went ahead, took a gamble, and chose as the programme for the day 'All the Beethoven symphonies.' It seemed, as he said, "a suitably ridiculous challenge." However, such well-loved works were probably just the best choice he could have made, and contrary to the received wisdom that people would certainly be too busy doing other things at this time, lots of people turned up. Each of the Cobweb regional groups was responsible for one symphony —with one left over, obviously-since Beethoven wrote nine, -but on the day many of the assembled band took part in considerably more than their allotted one. In fact some saw it as a matter of honour to play all nine. Someone did suggest that we should seek sponsorship per symphony, but sadly that idea was not taken up. A pity, as we could have made a packet for orchestra funds!

One of the benefits of Middlesbrough Town Hall is the vast amount of space available including the Crypt, where a running buffet was made available, along with a children's corner and yes, a fund-raising raffle.

Whether our Director's fond hope that "participants will have the chance to experience from the inside Beethoven's development from talented youngster to mature genius" was really appreciated amidst the torrent of notes and a considerable amount of sight-reading, one leaves to the imagination, but speaking as one who took part, it was a truly wonderful day, and an inspired idea.

All bright Cobweb ideas are of course destined to be repeated, and so Easter Bank Holiday 2012 saw the orchestra assembled in Middlesbrough again, this time to play as many overtures as possible in the time available. These ranged from Mozart to McCunn, and from Schubert to Shostakovich (that very loud *Festival Overture* again!), not forgetting John Williams' Jurassic Park and the rousing ending, which could only be Tchaikovsky's 1812.

Perhaps the most successful Big Play day to date, has been that of 2013, when we gave an opportunity to all the budding soloists in the orchestra to play that solo they have had under their hats for so many years and were just longing to be able to play with an orchestra. Indeed there was scarcely enough time to fit them all in, and certainly not enough time to eat, drink, socialise AND take part in the many fund-raising activities organised by the various groups. Peter and Ruth's Big Concertos Quiz obviously took ages to compile, but there was just so little time. The intense cold inside the hall was forgotten, it was an absolute joy to hear the very able playing of violins, clarinets, and trumpets (to mention only a few) and a privilege to accompany them.

"What a sensational day was had by us all- shattered but happy!"
"Absolutely beautiful solo-playing. What talent there is in the Cobweb Orchestra."
"I wanted to do it all again as I'd just warmed up!"
"What a feat of organisation- so well organised AND fun!"

What will Andy choose next time, we wonder?

Performing for the Queen Summer 2012.

The Cobweb orchestra never ceases to amaze by what it gets itself involved in. We didn't envisage getting mixed up with the Jubilee celebrations apart from the usual summer Proms in the Park gig at Auckland Castle, though even this proved interesting this year, as we were asked to accompany Joe McElderry in a couple of his numbers- this didn't actually happen as Joe proved one person who couldn't quite cope with Cobwebs, for whatever reason!

Then one day we were invited to play for no less a person than the Queen herself at the opening of the new White Water Centre at the Tees Barrage, and Andy was suddenly busy composing a piece specially for the occasion. Such an auspicious event cannot go unrecorded – at length- and so here is Hilda Sim's account from the Summer 2012 newsletter.

"I don't usually suffer from nerves but was feeling jittery en route to Stockton on Wednesday July 18th. Due to technical constraints we were restricted to wind instruments only- which turned out to be apt for the weather conditions. Sorry, strings, we really did miss you!

The Big Day arrived. Police were ubiquitous, the site had been hermetically sealed and security guards were manning the barricades. After some tense negotiations we were admitted and issued with security wrist- bands. Our leader Andy was given a special badge engraved with his name, and (curiously) "Cob-Webb".

Excitement mounted. With disbelief I heard I was one of the three lucky names pulled out of the orchestra hat to meet the Queen, along with Rye (bassoon) and Steve (French horn).

Sue and Andy had done a lot of organisation in advance. For example we were allocated a Portakabin "Green Room" with our own private pair of loos.

The band trooped up to the stage for a rehearsal on a peninsula surrounded by foaming waters. Overnight rain had blown under the canopy and soaked the seat cushions so we were issued with black bin liners which looked rather fetching draped over the chairs. Scudding purple clouds of imminent rain raced across the sky threatening another soaking, so to counter the gusting breezes we fastened music to the stands with clothes pegs, some improvised rubber bands, and Ingenious Andrew used giant magnets (Forsyth's Foresight!).

While we played Sousa's Liberty Bell Andy went walkabout; and on returning warned us that the audience would hear every wrong note through the sound system, so- if in doubt, leave it out! The only piece that the Queen was actually going to hear was Maestro Andy Jackson's own piece, 'White

Water Music', specially commissioned and composed for the occasion, and there was instant endorsement from a sound engineer whistling the tune after we had rehearsed it- surely a good omen.

Back at the Green Room, poor Andy's *al fresco* briefing was upstaged by the merry antics of police sniffer dog, Nippy, who happily ignored his frustrated handler shouting "Here!" and "Come back!" Nippy particularly relished checking out our portaloos.

We trooped back up onto the stage for the local TV news to film us in action, but that idea was abandoned and so, like the Grand Old Duke of York's men, we marched back down again. Time passed. We waited. Nerves jangled. At last though, we got the call- To the Stage!

Buses from the Park and Ride had brought in five thousand people, including several of our own eminent string players with guest tickets. Spectators were spread over the grassy bank watching canoeists cavorting on the swirling rapids. Walkways were lined with chattering children waving Union Jacks. We played our first set, including Handel's Water Music, and Machines by Stephanie Cant.

The compere was a well-known TV star of yonder years. With perfect timing, when Her Majesty The Queen and His Royal Highness the Duke of Edinburgh arrived the rain clouds evaporated and the sun shone with glorious warmth. We played Walton's 'Crown Imperial' while they raised the Royal Standard.

Flyer for course that started it all.
Flyer for first concert.
Cobweb Fundraising Cookery Book.

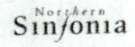

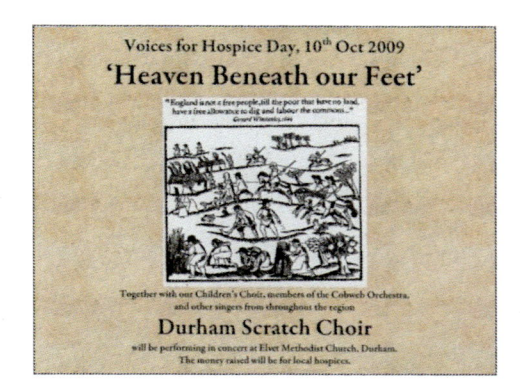

Three promotional posters.
Cobweb Orchestra card designed by Rosemary Chapman.

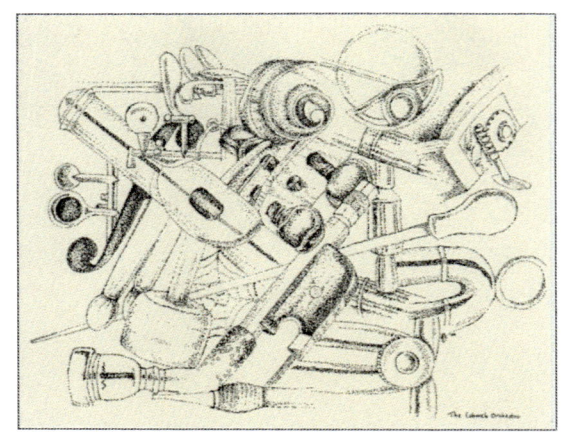

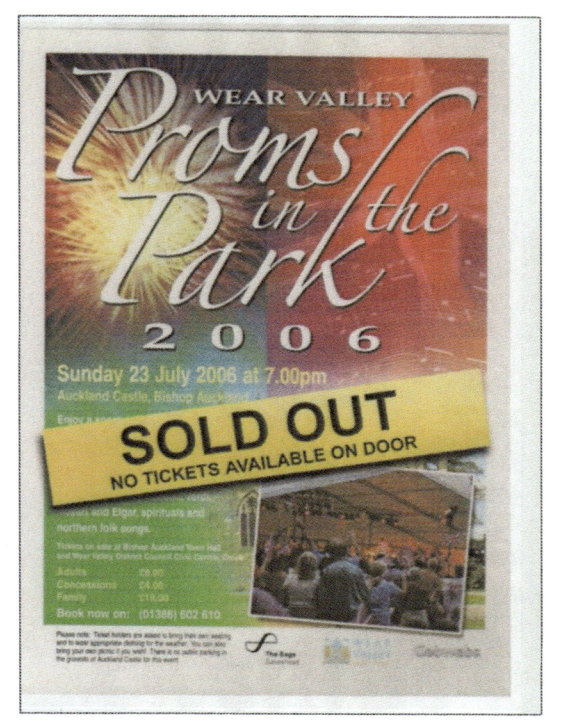

Cobweb fundraising card designed by Barbara Griffin for Teesside group.

Promotional posters from 2006 and 2009.

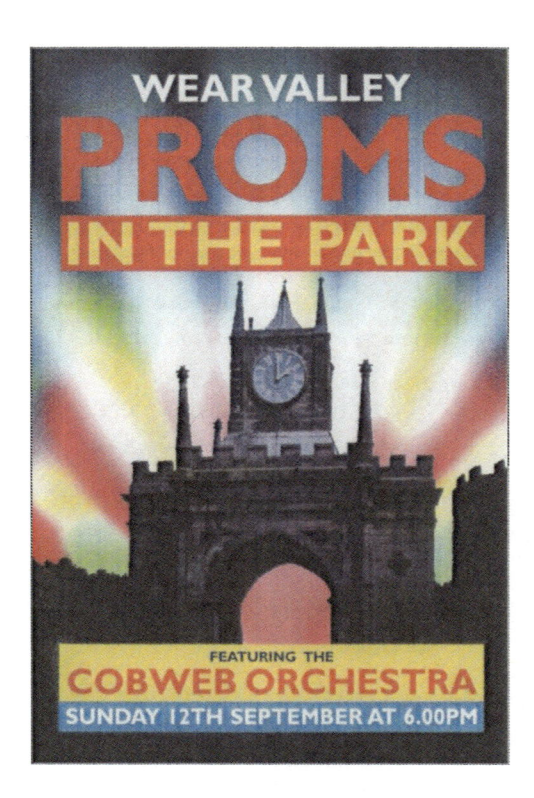

Three more promotional posters.
Andy receiving epic award from Minister Ed Vaisey in 2011.

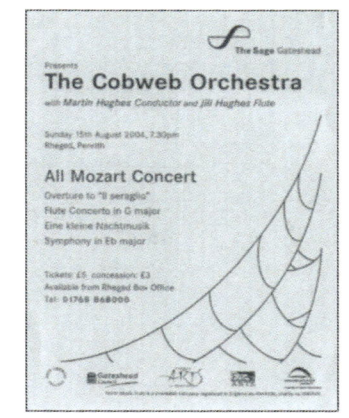

Gospel Requiem The Sage Gateshead 27/11/05   photo by Kit Jackson

200 musicians on stage in Hall 1 of Sage Gateshead for the Gospel Requiem in October 2005.

Orchestra's 10th Birthday Party at Hexham.

Helen Pyburn tries her hand at conducting at Sedbergh Residential.

The Cabaret Group.

Pause for a photo call at Sedbergh Residential.

Catherine Shackell conducting the York Group.

Sun goes to the heads of musicians on the Tuscany trip 2009, but no instruments came to harm!

Tuscany group 2011 with guest tutor Stephen Reay from Northern Sinfonia.

There was an anti-climax while the Queen went into a marquee for a natter with the VIPs. Would she have a cuppa, or a chance to wash her hands? A swan landed on the grass near a crowd barrier and rested there for the duration. Suddenly the crowd was watching the big screen again as the Queen emerged and began her Royal Progress. She was wearing an ensemble in bright apricot, easy to see from afar. The hat must have been firmly wedged on with hatpins or Velcro to prevent lift-off in the strong south-westerlies.

In my position as Deputy 4th Principal 5th trumpet, I got a grandstand view as the Queen pressed the Big Red Button to open the sluice gates. Escorting the Queen, the Chief Executive of Stockton Borough Council leapt several feet in the air as she triggered the crashing explosion, but the Queen and Prince Philip stood rock steady. A tidal wave surged down the channel, bearing more canoes and firemen in survival kit rescued a man from atop a floating car.

The Royal entourage sat only twenty feet from us while we played Andy's superb composition. There was rapturous applause. The Queen and Philip carried on clapping after everyone else had stopped. Maybe they were having a 'last clap' contest.

A plaque was unveiled while yet more canoeists carried flares through the frothy deluge. Then the Duke marched over to chat with the flutes (Andrew, Chrissie and Claire), Jude (saxophone) and Richard (horn). He asked about the clothes pegs... possibly thinking of new ways for his wife to keep her hat on? The Queen greeted us with a delicate handshake. She was wearing black gloves and a surprising amount of make-up. She asked if it was difficult to play in the wind. We pointed out the clothes pegs. She didn't mention James Bond or helicopters.

The Queen and Duke drove off in the Royal car, possibly discussing new uses for clothes pegs. Even the republicans amongst us were moved by the Royals. What a Day to Remember- surreal, but a lot of fun! I felt tremendously privileged to be part of the White Water Event- another outstanding Cobweb occasion.

And then…

Cobwebs at the Flame Celebration.

While one group of Cobwebbers were enjoying the sunshine of Dachau in summer 2012, another was invited to take part in a pre-Paralympics event at Beamish Museum, to celebrate the arrival of a splinter of the English Olympic flame on its tour round the country before being combined with the Paralympic flame in London. A small group of around twenty-four players had to squeeze itself onto the bandstand at Beamish, and played a programme under the baton of Clarence Adoo which included a new work specially composed for the occasion by Andy, called 'Paraflame.' Other works on the subject of 'fire and flame' were included, 'Chariots of Fire', Handel's Fireworks music, you can guess…

6. Significant Others: stories of some of those left behind – or not

There have been many people ranging from the professional musicians of the Sinfonia and elsewhere, to sponsors, administrators, fund-raisers and well-wishers of all kinds who have contributed to the Cobweb phenomenon. What of those we leave behind when we come to sessions, workshops and weekends, not to mention residentials? Far from just enjoying a few hours of peace and quiet at home, coming along as taxi drivers, or even tagging along on foreign jaunts, the 'Cobweb effect' works out in different ways for a selection of our nearest and dearest.

Here is just a sample of contributions.

From our Webmaster, Colin Reed:

"The Cobweb orchestra has been part of my life since my wife joined when it was formed in 1995. It has brought us a lot of pleasure since then, particularly when the orchestra played at our wedding in 1998. Being unable to play a musical instrument myself meant that the only way I was able to help the orchestra in the past was by transporting players and attending as many performances as possible. But I wanted to do more.

Developing the website could be compared to composing a piece of music. Each has its own language and rules and as I have discovered, they are equally addictive. What started as a lunchtime work project culminated in early starts and spending another hour or two on it once the working day had finished. I was quite disappointed when I had to take a week's holiday to move house!"

The Cobweb Ghost. Sue Kane. (written in 2002)

"I am a Cobweb ghost of six years. A fly on the wall. Never been to a Cobwebs Workshop, only managed a couple of concerts, yet I know all about dramatic car journeys looking for obscure church halls, hunting for missing sections of orchestral scores. I know that opportunities have been created and desires met, instruments bequeathed and then recalled when the owner understands that expertise and age are no barrier to rediscovering the pleasure of playing. I know about the seemingly endless commitment for all day workshops followed by a concert. Sleeping in Youth Hostels, yuk. Performing in freezing cold venues, encouraging six-year-old violinists.

From my privileged position here on the wall, I get a buzz from all that activity. The enthusiasm for bizarre projects like 'Conductors' Days', of all things. Invigorating, passionate and joyful performances. I am sure that I am only one of the many hangers-on to the strands of your infectious web."

Becoming entangled in the Web. Ruth Tanner.

"When my son gave up playing his cello in favour of the double bass, and I expressed my disappointment, he said: "If you're so keen on the cello, Mum, play it yourself!" Well, I was in my mid-fifties, had had a wonderful musical life in singing, and married to an organist. Was it possible? It was something I really regretted, never having played an orchestral instrument, and experienced the 'wow' of being part of an orchestra.

Number One Son then surrendered his cheap East European bass for a better one, and so there was now a bass lying around at home too. Organist husband decided that his retirement project to learn to play the double bass might as well be advanced, and somehow discovered the Cobweb Orchestra. So began the transformation of the 'solitary megalomaniac' in his organ loft into a sociable member of a very sociable orchestra, making disgustingly fast progress on the bass without a single lesson - (it must be like being naturally sporty!) It did take a while to get used to listening to the Cobwebs - they didn't always make a truly great sound, but they did seem to be having enormous fun! (But that was before I 'got it'.) I sang in the Choral Symphony in Van Mildert, went to 'Sell-By' because I was a member of the WEA, whose tutor had been responsible for the libretto, and heard Roberto Carillo-Garcia play the Rodrigo Guitar Concerto because Brian had told me how fantastic it was to stand beside him in the bass rank - just like a tutorial. But still I didn't quite have the confidence…

I went to an Absolute Beginners' Day in Berwick and was convinced that I was the ONLY beginner there for sure. I think I must have looked rather wild-eyed and pale by the end, as I remember Andy very sympathetically saying "I know, it all just rushes past you doesn't it?" It most certainly did! I ran away and did an OU French course instead.

Then in 2005 we went to the Tuscany Summer School, Hubby as a player, myself (as I thought) as an 'accompanying person.' What do you know? There happened to be a spare cello lying there. I toyed with a few notes of the lovely SLOW *Lachrimae* and other suitably simple pieces. The rest, as they say, is history. Cobwebs had launched me! I came home, found a good teacher, worked very hard to make up for 40 wasted years not playing the cello, and now attend Cobwebs more than the other half, who plays his bass in other orchestras too - and still hasn't retired!"

Observations of a Tolerant Husband. Gerry Blackwell

"My wife has always been keen on music-listening, attending concerts, singing and playing. As a youngster she learnt to play the piano, clearly enjoying the challenge and experience, but career, marriage and children curtailed musical involvement for a few years. However, the pause saw a growing desire to widen musical participation beyond the comparatively isolated position at the keyboard. An ambition to play a stringed instrument in company had always been present in her, and was realised through the dual opportunity afforded by the accessibility of both lessons and a school orchestra that welcomed adult players. Her choice of instrument was the 'cello (in no small part due to the heroine-status of Jacqueline du Pre at the time) and in a short time she was happily engaged having a regular lesson, practising assiduously and being an increasingly important member of the school orchestra in rehearsals and concerts. A social dimension soon became apparent, and the 'cello section were regularly entertained to much appreciated and convivial dinners, forming deep friendships that have reached far beyond the confines of school days.

Whilst by no means scorning these initial playing opportunities, awareness of the existence, intentions and ambitions of the Cobweb Orchestra stimulated much interest. From the start the meetings at Tebay provided enormous pleasure, opening up new social as well as musical interests. For the last few years, Tuesday evenings have seen an early supper and a seven o'clock departure from Sedbergh, generally regardless of the weather, travel up the motorway to Exit 38 and thence to the Methodist Hall in Tebay. The return at 10 o'clock has been accompanied by animated accounts of the music played, standard achieved, news of participants and details of plans for the future.

As a husband it has been a delight to witness this involvement. Rarely with "increasing maturity" do such opportunities arise, but Cobwebs has provided them. Of late, the delights and challenges have extended far beyond Tebay, with regular trips to Tuscany and concerts in Germany, with remarkable friendships being made. Weekends of concentrated playing and days devoted to honing skills and confronting new challenges abound. Besides, being part of an organisation that has received national recognition for its innovative approach to Community music making, and the opportunity to perform in the Sage Gateshead and meet distinguished figures from the world of music is a valued bonus.

One might wonder why a husband who is uninvolved personally should write with such enthusiasm. The answer is twofold: it is delightful to see one's wife enjoying this aspect of life so much. The second reason is more self-centred. The adage "If you can't beat them join them" comes into play. I was inclined on my retirement to satisfy an envy that had been with me for years. Musicians clearly had a great love for their activities and gained much fulfilment, an experience closed to me, whose musical experience had never gone beyond singing in the choral society and following whoever sang the loudest near me, regardless of part.

Fortunately a brass band was resurrected in Sedbergh just coinciding with my retirement. It became defunct in 1914 and was brought back into being by a group who had never had the chance to play in their youth. Whilst there has been no fairy tale ending - I am not the leading baritone horn soloist in the Black Dyke Mills band - I am a very contented second baritone horn player – (there is no third desk, else...)- in a very active Sedbergh Brass Band that has some twenty public engagements a year and has, since its formation visited Slovenia, Italy and Belgium, besides making CDs in Blackpool and Dumfries. Thus it can be said that I have every reason to be grateful to the Cobweb Orchestra. Whilst not one of those who has taken out a neglected instrument from the attic and blown away the Cobwebs, I have been stimulated to immerse myself in a similar musical experience."

There are, of course, numerous others of significance who have helped to make the Cobweb project what it is.

It was the initial enthusiasm of Martin Weston, Arts Officer with Derwentside District Council at the time, for a new type of orchestra, plus Derwentside's seed-funding that made the development of the orchestra, the network, the newsletter and various other spin-off events possible. We have held numerous concerts in the Lamplight Theatre in Stanley, including the first Voices for Hospices choral event, the first performance of *'Sell-By'*, plus many others, and we are truly grateful for Martin's continuing support.

Friends from the Northern Sinfonia

Iona Brown's delightful and talented presence with the orchestra dates from as early as the noted Mahler 1 Challenge in Alnwick in January 1997 and she has joined us on several other occasions as coach and as soloist, memorably (twice now) in the beautiful Max Bruch Violin Concerto. As early as February and March 1997, Mike Gerrard, Principal viola with the Northern Sinfonia, came along to help with some Beethoven workshops in Peterlee. His involvement was much appreciated and by March the following year, Mike featured as soloist with the orchestra in Berlioz's "Harold in Italy," a concert conducted by founder friend, (and therefore NOT "other"!) Chris Griffiths. This concert took place in the Civic Centre, Stanley, again with support from the Derwentside District Council plus sponsorship from Marks and Spencer.

Reports from the event included comments from Martin Weston: "A superb final concert," from Mark Monument of Northern Arts: "I thoroughly enjoyed myself.- It was good to see such effort, commitment and drive, not to mention the generous assistance from those Northern Sinfonia players supporting the whole edifice from the back desks," and from Chris Griffiths himself: "It never fails to amaze me how a performance can really take off as it certainly seemed to in Stanley."

Then in 2007 Iona and Mike came together to Tuscany when the string players revelled in the "free" tuition they received, and where Mike claimed he was now a true Cobwebber as he tried his hand at conducting for the first time. His vigorous conducting as he tried to haul us through the intricacies of Holst's *"St. Paul's Suite"* gave us some cause for concern, as his face grew ever redder in the Italian heat. We also gained a healthy respect for the abilities of the St. Paul's Girls' School pupils.

Stephen Reay (described in a newsletter as the Sinfonia's "charismatic bassoonist") also began his involvement in the early days. In 1997 Stephen did some coaching with a wind quintet, in Summer 2000 he made his debut as a conductor in the "Year of Loud Music" concert by the lake at Keswick, and by 2009 he was also tempted to act as resident tutor at the Tuscany residential, which he (and we) enjoyed so much that he returned for the next one. Stephen also adds to the quality of the Cobweb experience by teaching at least one of our regular bassoonists, Sheila Ryan.

Another much treasured Northern Sinfonia friend is Clarence Adoo. Clarence has been involved for many years, leading brass sectionals at bigger events, popping in to listen to some of our study days, using us on one memorable afternoon as guinea pigs as he tried out his 'dalek' stick for conducting. Over the years Cobwebs has played host to many conductors each with their own foibles. Clarence however is the only one we know who literally "uses his head."

Clarence was one of the UK's top trumpeters, playing also alongside artists such as Courtney Pine, before a car crash in 1995 left him paralysed from the shoulders down. When asked by Libby Purves on Radio 4 about his reaction to his life changing injuries, Clarence acknowledged the help his Christian faith had given him and said; "I've got a choice, really. One is to give up and feel sorry for myself. Or the other attitude is to be positive and dust myself down and have a good crack at life and see what is possible."

How, you might wonder, does someone paralysed from the shoulders down conduct an orchestra? There's no waving of arms or dancing about on the podium. All instructions come from head and face movements - the 'dalek' baton is still around but tends to hinder our reading of what Clarence is wanting to communicate, so that when he put it on and asked "How do I look?" our response was "Silly!"

As well as conducting workshops and occasionally standing in for Andy at the Sage group on Wednesdays, Clarence has the opportunity once again to make music for himself. He now plays "Headspace", a wind instrument controlled by breath and devised for him by German conductor and composer Rolf Gehlhaar. With this instrument Clarence has become a founder member of the Paraorchestra, a band founded by Charles Hazelwood, the conductor and radio and television presenter, for musicians with various types of disability. In 2012 they were asked to play at the closing ceremony of the Paralympics, and just before the Paralympics, a documentary was shown on Channel 4 about the orchestra, featuring Clarence among others. In preparation for this, he asked the Cobweb orchestra to play and be filmed with him- in Hall 1 of The Sage. So it was that on 21st May a small group performed Beethoven's *'Coriolan'* overture under Clarence's direction, (though not with his baton) whilst being filmed from every direction for what seemed like a very long time.

In the event, though we were delighted to see Clarence feature largely in the programme, the orchestra, as is the way with films, had about ten seconds of exposure, featuring one of our ace horn players and our intrepid percussionist, Pauline. We were of course delighted to have even been involved in supporting Clarence in this venture and always look forward to his silently gliding into our rehearsals.

There are so many other present and former Sinfonia players to whom we owe debts of gratitude: Jeanette Mountain, from her early cello workshops in 2000, to coming round the libraries in a coach with us one Saturday, and for an Elgar *Cello Concerto* performance, where she shared the solo spotlight with Howard Rocke and Andrew Cottrell. Roberto Carillo-Garcia not only conducted the orchestra in Keswick and inspired with his double-bass playing, but also gave a memorable performance of the Rodrigo *Guitar Concerto*. We even aspired to inviting the Allegri Quartet to give a workshop followed by a joint concert with us in 1999.

Although a company rather than an individual, Marks and Spencer certainly figure in our history as "significant others" because their 5-year sponsorship not only supported several editions and a definite upgrading of our newsletter, but also enabled the setting up of the two new groups in Northumberland and Cumbria in 1998 and 1999 respectively. In 1999 a concert in an M&S store was planned by way of a "thank you."

Anthony Sargent, General Manager of The Sage Gateshead has worked with us for ten years, conducting workshops and performances, and also producing 2 CDs. Why, let alone how, does this busy person find time to do it? The sleeve notes to the CDs he has been involved with suggest the reason.

He describes the Bizet *Symphony in C* as "an ideal Cobweb piece - full of character, tricky enough to be interesting but not impossibly hard for the Cobwebs' unique 'all-comers welcome' approach, and bursting with just the same extravagant joy that the Cobweb players themselves bring to their playing."

Of the Mozart CD he wrote "I hope you will pick up from the CD something of those unique Cobweb qualities: discovery and adventure, courage and joy". What a wonderful accolade!

Late news! We were delighted to hear that Anthony had received a CBE in the Queen's Birthday Honours list in 2013. Also the Northern Sinfonia became the Royal Northern Sinfonia. We congratulate them both on these well-deserved accolades.

During Summer 2013 we were sad to hear of the death of Alan Jones, husband of Liz Carlile. Alan had been a keen Cobweb beginner on the viola, never failing to point out what a complete rookie he was, as he even had to learn to read the dots! I will treasure a session with him when we struggled along with some Very Easy Pieces for viola and cello by Elgar. I think we encouraged each other by the mutually elementary standard of our playing. Alan's real enjoyment was with the Durham Scratch Choir when his eyes glowed with enthusiasm as he sang along. A constant and loyal support to Liz during her time as Librarian and the Administrator, he was, as Liz says, "a lovely man".

7. Residentials - "A Long Weekend of Music Making with no Distractions"

The Cobweb timetable had soon come to include weekend workshops as well as the weekly evening meetings, so the logical extension of this was to experiment with the idea of a whole weekend 'residential.' The first was in 2000 at the Brewery Arts Centre in Kendal, Cumbria.

The idea of a longer period of time together, "a long weekend of music-making with no distractions" as someone described it, gave more time for working on pieces, and exploring new types of music in smaller groups. By this time there were three Cobweb groups in rather far-flung parts of the region: Harelaw (Durham), Newbiggin (Northumberland), and Tebay in Cumbria, so this gave people from all the groups a chance to meet up to play and to get to know each other better. Sixty two players attended, with ages ranging from 10 to over 80.

"What a weekend," wrote Marj Baillie. "We seemed to get through an enormous amount of repertoire and I really enjoyed the varied nature of the things we did. I even enjoyed improvising when singing on Sunday….I now love the unpredictability of things which always seem to work out well in the end. When are we doing it again?"

The Kendal residential was repeated twice more, and by the third year the pattern had settled into 'the usual menu of rehearsals, sectionals, scratch sessions, ensembles, improvising and socialising,'- such a tightly filled schedule that already it was a case of 'so much to do, so little time,' and the idea of the Cobweb residential was here to stay.

At the third weekend in 2002, Boriana Nakeva was invited back after two successful concerts with the orchestra the previous Autumn, to work with the group. The weather this particular year was not so kind, however, and this was when the vision of a summer meeting in Tuscany was born (see Ch. 8).

In 2003, the Spring residential moved to Kielder, a very quiet (till we arrived!) village at the head of Kielder Water in Northumberland, where again, through the good offices of Sue Baker, who worked for the YHA, the whole youth hostel was taken over. Such was the reputation of these weekends that all the rooms were soon taken. Some people chose to stay at a nearby hotel in Falstone, which despite the peaceful surroundings and beautiful views, is most memorable for being the only hotel known to the writer where a hot water bottle was necessary. By this time even more new musical styles were being explored, including acoustic jazz sessions and folk music, and tutors Jo Green, David Oliver and Paul Beck all came along to help Andy. Once again it sounds as if there would be barely enough time to fit in all the activities planned.

"Wasn't it great- AGAIN! So much to do, so many friends, old and new, so many challenges and such rewards!"

Kielder hosted the Spring residential for the next three years. The 2005 weekend was pronounced the "best yet." Could it have been that, contrary to normal custom, and due to a change of programming during the winter, the key work for the weekend, Dvorak's 7th *Symphony*, was revealed in advance thus giving people the chance to practise?

By 2005 an experimental non-residential weekend was held in Kirby Stephen, a central point nestling in the hills between Cumbria and the North East. Several Tebay Cobwebbers lived nearby so the weekend was a mix of those coming for individual days, going home and returning, or making their own arrangements to stay overnight. This was pronounced another success. Such was the appetite for weekend playing that in July of the same year, Andy reported that yes, indeed, people were commenting that at the Kielder residential there was 'never enough time' for chamber groups to get together to play. What had actually happened was that the opportunity had been given for the first time for many to sample this smaller, more intimate form of music making, and the response was enormous. As Liz Carlile wrote in the same newsletter, "Suddenly, among Cobwebs there seems to be a surge of string players playing chamber music."

So Andy booked Ridley Hall in Northumberland and what has become another regular event in the late autumn calendar was born. This was not to replace Kielder but to provide something different, less structured and requiring a bigger organisational input from participants. There was a small proportion of pre-organised music-making but for the rest this must have been something of an act of faith on the part of the leaders. However, it all worked out well, and people were able to find the 'rest of their quartets' or other appropriate grouping. Pauline Holbrook reported that "for those of us not used to playing in smaller ensembles it was a valuable opportunity to explore a new type of music, made very enjoyable by the tolerance and encouragement of more experienced players. Some groups had pre-set agendas, while others formed ad-hoc throughout the weekend."

After the 2006 Ridley Hall weekend Anita Arris wrote: "I was quite apprehensive about going on the Ridley Hall weekend having only been part of Cobwebs since September, and only having started playing the oboe in January. However, everyone made me feel very welcome and I surprised myself by being able to play more than I expected. It was encouraging talking to people who said they too had come along in the past with little experience but had just played what they could. I felt I could join in and it didn't matter if I only played one or two notes."

After the weekend in 2012, Ian Robertson wrote from the point of view of an Accompanying Person: "The structure of the weekend is quite outstanding, the work that Andy puts in is unstinted and the dedication and enthusiasm of all participants is infectious. Even I, the biggest non-joiner of all, become captivated. What matter if I cannot tell a treble clef from a dotty crotchet? Nobody minds, but if I really want to know someone is sure to explain with kindness and courtesy.

Perhaps the best way to explain the transformation is to describe the day today. Gradually a drift develops in the direction of the lovely rehearsal room where Andy is already active among the players as they settle to their places and instruments. My vantage point-a little alcove half way up the stairs enables me to hear and sometimes, see, Andy at work. At first the noise is pretty awful and he patiently sorts out the individual problems and steers his willing group into shape. Gradually the music emerges from the noise, and I know I have heard it before somewhere…. How satisfying to hear such a lovely musical construction being drawn out from an assembly of so many and such varied folk.

Now the melody changes to something I have never heard before. In no time at all it begins to sound most attractive to my ear; under its benign influence all sorts of fresh ideas begin to flow towards my stale uninteresting rambling tale,- my 'work'.. By the time the music comes to a flourishing finale, my work has also transformed itself into something that I feel has got some sort of future, and I too am infected with the surrounding excitement and happiness. I am already a part of the scene, no longer apart from it."

The value of residentials had definitely been proved and in December 2005 a questionnaire was included in the newsletter looking for ideas and suggestions regarding venues and type of accommodation. In the Summer of 2007 another non-residential weekend was held, this time in Sedbergh, a peaceful small market town nestling on the western side of the Howgills and dominated by Sedbergh School. A former employee of the school, Sheila Blackwell, also a regular member of the Tebay group, was the host and inspiration for this trial run. It proved to be another great success and so after four years in the 'far north' of Kielder, the Spring residential moved to Sedbergh School, where it has remained ever since.

The Sedbergh residentials have seen a wide variety of activities, including some unusual, if not downright whacky, Sunday mornings. For a while, Andy thought it would be instructive for players to change instruments, which gave rise to such sights as Tracy attempting to play the double bass, Brian on the cymbals and great hilarity all round, plus a greater appreciation of the intricacy and the challenge of other people's instruments. One year we had a Health and Safety orchestra, where ear muffs, helmets etc. were worn. We have attempted some wonderful works, including Catherine leading us through the whole of Smetana's *Ma Vlast*, (not just *Vltava*) and Brian seizing the opportunity to play the school organ in the Saint-Saëns *Symphony No 3,* also known as the *Organ Symphony*. Catherine also led us through a session on Minimalist music, which was interesting and instructive. Saturday evenings have traditionally been given over to a Concert Party, when individuals have entertained us with their party pieces, which may well have been the inspiration for the Soloists' Big Play day at Middlesbrough.

The latest departure, in Summer 2013, was a chamber orchestra weekend, where a smaller group of around 26 players met to play the early classics and pieces intended for a more intimate sound, pretty well just like the original repertoire of the Northern Sinfonia. The weekend was amazing, with glorious weather and a remote location at Blackton Grange between Hury and Balderhead reservoirs in Teesdale where we could make as much noise as we liked for as long as we wanted. Music ranged from Cimarosa to Ravel, (the *Tombeau de Couperin* proving surprisingly tricky), with symphonies by Mozart and Schubert, and not forgetting John Hawkes' *Divertimento.* Such was the success of the weekend, crowned by wonderful catering by Sue Baker, that it is unlikely to have been a one-off. It seems likely to become yet another regular event to squeeze into the Cobwebs' busy schedule.

8. Global Connections "Enjoying Sounds"

Making an impact internationally predates Cobweb visits abroad by some years.
"Playing with Cobweb Orchestra is a wonderful experience. I will miss you all very much when I go back to Japan."

So wrote Miki Shintomi after a year playing with the orchestra in 1999. She wrote again on her return to Japan:

"I miss you all. I was so happy to see you all and play lovely music together. I hope your orchestra keeps going well. I was impressed that you were enjoying music very much. We sometimes forget it, only 'practise and practise.' The Japanese characters for music mean 'enjoying sounds.' It is true. I hope I'll play viola with you again."

"It makes you want to tap your Hands."

An audience member at the Newbiggin concert in September 1999, Neeru Tandon, wrote about his first "live" Western concert:

"I don't know what I expected - something like the Last Night of the Proms. It sounded better! I liked being so close and able to see everyone and figure out where the sound was coming from. I especially liked the violins and the percussionist - he obviously enjoyed what he was doing. I preferred the Mozart: it was more gentle, soothing and calm. The Tchaikovsky was vibrant. Of course I knew some of the music from adverts and films. I couldn't compare Indian and Western music. It is very different, and I enjoy both. Tell me when you have your next concert."

Tuscany

The tradition of residentials had become a regular part of Cobwebs' activities since the first weekend away in Kendal in 2001. This was so successful that it was repeated for two more years, with equal success musically, though dogged by bad weather.

It was during one of the Kendal weekends that Andrew Forsyth first broached the idea of a summer trip to Tuscany to play music, sunbathe, swim and partake of good food and wine, and unsurprisingly the idea was taken up with enthusiasm. Indeed, the venue, and the format for that well researched week in 2003 was so successful that it has hardly changed since. There have been some additions squeezed into the schedule, such as cookery lessons, evening ceilidhs and small instrumental groups who practice in corners while others (are trying to) rest or take a swim. Our host, Giulia, has always been attentive and understanding of our needs, not to mention tolerant of the noise we make, sometimes late into the night! (Fortunately Il Grande Prato is well out of town up on top of a hill.) She also helps to fix up and liaise with our concert venues and always attends our concerts and translates Andy's introductions.

Andrew recalls how an idea floated in a pub on a chilly February night in Cumbria turned into a biennial Cobweb highlight for those lucky enough to be able to go.

"The germ of an idea for an overseas trip was hatched in the pub in Kendal in February 2002. We were taking a break during a Cobweb Orchestra residential at the Brewery Arts Centre and our guest soloist was Bulgarian violinist Boriana Nakeva who was now living in Florence. Sitting shivering, with her scarf wound tightly round her neck and collar turned up, Boriana was clearly not impressed with the British weather.

I heard myself saying something along the lines of, "we should be doing this under the Tuscan sun, amongst the olive groves" at which several pairs of eyes lit up and the rabbit was, so to speak, off. That little seed had sprouted and some initial research suggested there may be some real possibilities. Over the following months, after an initial show of hands at Annfield Plain revealed strong support for the project, I made contact with over 100 accommodation providers in Tuscany to find which of them would welcome an orchestra, whilst providing a rehearsal space; a degree of solitude so as not to upset any non-participants and also the essential topographical features that would ensure no-one was in any doubt as to where we might be staying.

One by one, each potential suitor was discarded until we were left with just one, *Il Grande Prato* in the administrative district of Firenze (Florence) and lying in the centre of the triangle formed by Firenze, Siena and Pisa above a little-known town called Castelfiorentino. Its owner, Giulia Perticucci was very helpful in fielding my questions about our particular requirements.

The next step was the vetting so with, dear reader, what you will realise was understandable reluctance, Andy Jackson and I made a quick trip to Italy in the following May half-term to see what *Il Grande Prato* had to offer. In a whistle-stop visit, we met priests and town council officials, checked out potential concert performance sites and, most importantly, tested out the accommodation and explored with Giulia all of our options. This was going to be perfect, and so with the costs agreed, a package was put together for the first overseas trip.

55 orchestra members and family signed up, necessitating spilling out into the local village and hotels and in August 2003 we all descended upon Tuscany to spread the Cobweb gospel beyond our shores. We had also made contact with the local (state-run) music school, who lent us a double-bass and timpani and sent along two of their local students to join us. What followed was a fantastic week of music-making, sight-seeing, fine food, and socialising by the open-air pool with the huge, extended musical family that is Cobwebs. The die was cast."

Sheila Blackwell continues the story of that first trip, recounting the pleasures and perils of exchanging chilly northern climes for the heat of an Italian summer:

"After weeks of organising, trying to learn some Italian and polish up those scales, we finally set off via Blackpool and Stansted, arriving in Pisa early in the morning. The first thing that struck us was the intense heat. Everywhere was dry and brown, bar the wonderful cypress trees, even the geraniums lying dead in their window boxes, under the deep blue cloudless sky. We were slightly disoriented on arrival from lack of sleep and hunger, but after a siesta and a swim in the gloriously cool pool, we awaited our fellow players. Our first dinner was a feast of Italian cooking, with lashings of wine, which set us up for a good night's sleep.

Singing before breakfast was a tall order for me. However, after a few exercises we launched into a Bulgarian (I think) folk song, and then it was on to rehearse with the orchestra. The non-players lounging by the pool over their paperbacks heard us play, shaking their heads in horror at the cacophony of sounds floating across from the rehearsal room. A lot of work was needed to get us playing in tune, a vital aspect of orchestral playing!

The afternoon rehearsal began as black clouds loomed overhead, the air intense with high humidity. Richard Best was reduced to playing in his swimming trunks, with a strange band round his head. It became darker and darker as we played on, so that extra lighting and an electric fan had to be brought in. Suddenly there was a huge flash of lightning and a clap of thunder, rain began to lash through the ventilation holes in the brick wall and music was sent flying by the wind. We played on until the loudest thunderclap and brightest lightning flash I had ever seen plunged us into complete darkness - except for Richard who calmly switched on his head lamp and continued to play - alone! Power came on and went off intermittently until we finally abandoned the rehearsal and scattered to various parts of the "campus", to drink wine, or otherwise amuse ourselves.

Friday came and we rehearsed furiously, punctuated by wonderful swims in the pool. What a glorious place for making music and having fun. The week seems to have slipped by so fast. Now for our first concert. We dined early, (no wine, though it was there!) left on the bus and arrived at the

Sanctuary of St. Verdiana in the town centre, a beautiful baroque church with overwhelming decoration, paintings and yet a great air of calm. The Vaughan Williams arrangement of *'Greensleeves'* sounded wonderful in the great acoustics, and the Corelli was magnificent, with baroque bowing duly remembered, bar one 'bum note'- a B natural, which caused a huge wince from conductor Andy (wasn't me!).

The final day is always hectic, with final rehearsal, packing, group photograph, this time with all those who were able in the pool - with their instruments, then a final swim before our last concert in Santa Maria a Chianni in Gambassi Terme, a splendid Romanesque building, starkly simple and pure in style, high on a hill overlooking Gambassi, a lofty and unadorned church compared with the one last night. After an inauspicious start following in the wake of a double wedding, and finding our audience already in place when we finally got in (hence no time to play through or test the acoustics) we managed a reasonably good performance so ending our week in a little bit of (hot) heaven."

The Tuscany trip seems to have become embedded in the calendar now as a biennial event but it has also meant we have developed the mechanism for taking our members further afield. The opportunity to fill those intervening years first came in 2006 thanks to the International Office at Durham County Hall, through whom a trip was organised to Szolnok, their twin town in Hungary.

David Wood takes up the story:

Cobwebs in Hungary – Excerpts from the Captain's Log, stardate 2006

Day 1: (Wednesday). The first problem was that because of a national airport security alert, all our musical instruments had to travel in the aircraft hold. The Easyjet check-in desk at Newcastle was invaded by 24 people with instruments ranging in size from double bass to piccolo. Many of us felt like anxious parents seeing off

children as instruments disappeared through the special scanner and someone commented that the double bass looked like a coffin going into a crematorium incinerator! The instruments would not be seen again until arrival in Budapest. The flight was, however, uneventful and all the instruments thankfully arrived intact.

We were met by our first guide/translator, Anita and a bus which took us from Budapest to Szolnok where we were eventually deposited at our hotel. The night was balmy and very dark. After three hours in an airborne aluminium tube, and one hour in a bus across a dark plain, we could have been anywhere!

Day 2: (Thursday). Ah, daylight! The motel, within 15 minutes' walk from Szolnok town centre, was a series of military-looking huts, with a nice patina of faded paintwork, ill-fitting windows and sometimes unreliable plumbing, but I didn't hear anyone complaining. There was a basic restaurant and bar, a terrace, and camping area with outside tables.

After breakfast a rehearsal was held in the hotel's function room. Following this we met our second guide/translator, Annamária. The bus took us into Szolnok where we were treated to a visit to a traditional Hungarian spa within the Hotel Tisza. The changing facilities were interesting – we were advised that ladies and men were separate. However, an elderly Hungarian lady was calmly getting dressed in the men's section when we arrived. Was she concerned? Not a bit!

Lunch at Szolnok County Hall was followed by a coach journey to Kunstenmárton, a small town about one hour to the south east of Szolnok. We can't have been far from the Romanian border but orientation was not easy. The Great Central Plain is very aptly named!

The reason for this journey turned out to be a real treat. The music school in Kunstenmárton was waiting for us, with the school orchestra producing a stunningly accurate performance of *Colonel Bogey* (the Malcolm Arnold arrangement, I think) as well as two other marches. The orchestra consisted entirely of wind, brass and percussion instruments, and this was the emphasis of the school, which had been in existence for ten years. Ferenc Szőke, the principal, was a horn player, hence the wind influence. There was much to interest us and much to discuss, despite the limitations of language. We were touched by their hospitality to us, which included a table full of food and drink!

That evening we gave our first concert. This was in the Kunstenmárton Hall of Culture. In reality, this was a larger-than-average village hall. It must be said, however, that Cobwebs received their best reception ever, with music school pupils whooping and cheering after every piece! They also indulged in a peculiar rhythmic handclapping, sounding to us rather like slow handclapping. It seemed to have different meanings depending on context. On this occasion it meant "more please". We were to encounter it again at the General Assembly the next morning, but on that occasion it would simply be polite appreciation, and definitely NOT a request for an encore. (Our guide, Annamária was quite emphatic on this point).

The return journey to Szolnok included a stop at "Convoy City", which tried to be an American-style diner but with Hungarian food. (Cold blackberry cream soup was a first for most of us). This was our second three-course meal of the day, and that's not counting the breakfast or the buffet laid on for us by the music school. A trend was being set!

At this restaurant we met Dr. Ildiki Ürmössy. It was she who was in charge of all the arrangements for our visit. Most of us got to bed around 11.30, with the prospect of an early start the next day.

Day 3: (Friday). Breakfast was at 7am, followed by a concert (at about 9.30am)

in the previously-visited hall as part of the General Assembly of Jász-Nagykun-Szolnok County's European celebration, (Hungary has been an E.U. member since 2004). This was quite a formal occasion. Hungarians seem to love speeches, and there were quite a few of them. There was universal agreement, at least among orchestra members, that we played pretty well here. Lunch was on the terrace of the Tisza Hotel (situated on the bank of the River Tisza). Three courses again, accompanied by a bombardment of conkers and acorns from the surrounding trees. Then back to the Motel for a further rehearsal in preparation for the (outdoor) afternoon concert.

Hild Square in Szolnok centre was the venue. There was a stage with a professional amplification and mixing set-up together with some festival stalls selling wine and other produce. The square was actually in a concrete shopping mall, with swirling winds. Everyone had remembered their clothes pegs! When we arrived, the preceding act was in full swing. Our first experience of Hungarian gypsy music! This was a trio (one violin, one viola-like instrument, and one double bass) who rejoiced in the name of "Borfalu Cigányzenekar muzsikál". They were pretty sensational, with a very interesting and unusual string technique, and we had to follow them!

We played the Hornpipe (a slightly chaotic version) from Handel's *Water Music* to an audience of about 120 as an intro. Then followed a prize-giving ceremony for children who had taken part in a postcard design competition. One by one they received their prizes, and one by one our audience slowly disappeared! We played a somewhat shortened programme to an audience of three Hungarian musicians! This was more like a typical Cobweb concert. Andy then threw in the towel, and we adjourned back to the motel for supper. (You guessed it, - three more courses).

The Cobwebs Hungarian concert-giving experience was thus concluded. This was, however, by no means the end of the visit, for our hosts had arranged a superb sightseeing programme for us the following day, which consisted largely of wine tasting, dancing to the popular tunes of local musicians and a visit to an impressive Romanesque church and ruined monastery in a place called Bélapátfalva. It lay in a very impressive location, beneath high limestone cliffs (which were actually man-made, as a result of quarrying) extending up to 815m at Belko Peak.

The janitor was anxious to lock up the church, since it was almost 5pm, but not until the Cobwebs choir had sung a lovely performance of *Amazing Grace* inside the ancient building. The janitor had apparently said to Anita, our guide, "I knew they were English. All the English like to sing in here."

We will each keep our memories of this visit, the hospitality which greeted us, the music, the superb diary arrangements, and the good company of our guides, just to name a few. The "Lonely Planet" guide to Hungary says this:

"Hungary is a heart-stealer; it will lure you back again and again to sample its rich wines, lounge in its thermal spas, gaze at its birdlife and make one more attempt to master its hermetic language." Could anyone argue with that?

Serendipity: The Cobweb Orchestra in Bavaria

Our good friend Antje Roser describes how she came to hear of Cobwebs and her growing involvement with the orchestra over the years.

How we met the Cobweb Orchestra

In 2006 our family came to live in Leeds for six months; our eldest daughter Svenja was studying in Germany. Soon we missed making music with other people and joined a tiny orchestra in Horsforth. One day in spring someone in the orchestra handed out a flyer for a study day in Ripon (Dvorak's "New World" symphony) organized by the Cobweb Orchestra. We discussed the flyer and marvelled at the idea of playing Dvorak just for fun on one day. What an adventure, what chutzpah! Let's join them! I signed all of us up; unfortunately it was too late to order the sheet music. "So what", Nikolai said, "they will be playing slowly and we are good at sight-reading". The day came, but we arrived late due to heavy traffic on the road. The kids felt uneasy, they hate coming late. Nevertheless, I insisted on going on because of the paid fee or –looking back – rather because I had an inkling that it would change our lives forever when we would meet you and finally we arrived at the venue.

We opened the door, faced a huge orchestra already playing and we all stood rooted to the ground for a few minutes: "They play at full speed! This is NOT a rehearsal!" Just a millisecond before we would have left, Tilman, the violist, was spotted by his viola pal from Horsforth; she waved frantically, so he went over and was welcomed by the other violists. Nikolai then disappeared into the cello section, and Antonia and I meekly looked for empty chairs in the last row of the second violins. A moment later we were part of a big orchestra, playing Dvorak, just for fun, without a clue, sight-reading *presto*! This is unheard of in Germany. Antonia later said: "I got goose-bumps while I was playing, thinking: I am playing Dvorak! In an orchestra! Just like that! It's a miracle!" I came to sit next to Joan Best, and liked her immediately. During lunch we met her husband Richard and that was the beginning of a wonderful friendship with them and the beginning of our relationship with the Cobweb Orchestra.

How we came to Tuscany in 2007

That was easy: By signing up for the Cobweb Orchestra newsletter in Ripon and applying for the Tuscany trip, when Andrew Forsyth announced it in winter 2007. It must have been a new and strange experience for him: a totally unknown German member of Cobwebs signing up her daughter Antonia and herself, claiming that the child has been playing the violin for 8 years. Then her brothers became jealous and wanted to join us, therefore Andrew got another e-mail from me signing up two more children, 17 and 16, reputedly playing viola and cello for 12 and 10 years. Later it turned out that Nikolai could not make it and I asked Andrew whether I could swap the cellist for another violinist, our eldest daughter Svenja AND a cello on top for one of the Cobweb cellists. He generously accepted the bargain - fortunately I never learned what he really was thinking of such a crazy family! We had a great time in Tuscany, enjoyed everyone's company, the singing at night, the long rehearsals (what a relief- these English musicians do sometimes rehearse!), the amazing concerts in small Italian churches and we learned a lot from Andy, Iona and Michael. We were all deeply touched by your openness, your friendliness, your generosity, and your tolerance. Some will remember Svenja's tiny swim suit and Tilman's special friend Tom. Tilman only agreed to come if his friend Tom could join us for the trip. I didn't dare to tell Andrew that we were at the brink of losing the violist as well; instead I paid the price for keeping the violist by taking care of four teenagers between 13 and 20. I still have very vivid memories of that week! Since we all liked you very much (the kids only in their non-sullen, non-pouting, not-crazy-behaving moments, but there were some of these moments, I can assure you, and they did/do like you!), it crossed my mind that it would be very sad if we just could meet all of you only every other year in Tuscany. The result was an invitation to the Orchestra to come to Dachau – if you organize trips to Tuscany, why not to Bavaria the other year? Andy called that 'Serendipity' – hence the title of this story.

How everyone came to Dachau for the first time in 2008

The first exchange of e-mails with Andy Jackson and Andrew Forsyth regarding the planning of the Cobweb trip to Bavaria began in January 2008. Soon it became clear that there are inter-cultural challenges: In Germany the students' dormitories are not rented out in the holidays, so we would have to find a hotel or other accommodation. There are no local radio stations that might be interested in events in their neighbourhood, so we would have to live without radio broadcasts about the Cobweb orchestra. The town's tourist office did not have any funds for foreign cultural messengers, so nobody would support us financially, and in most of the local mainly Catholic churches sacred music has priority even over beautiful Mozart symphonies. The local newspaper at least seemed to be interested in the story and sent a trainee, lovely Elizabeth, who did her best tocover all. All in all, we had to accept the special Bavarian way of doing things. Luckily, these obstacles did not prevent you from coming – sometimes I wondered whether you'd give up! Yet, on the contrary, Andrew patiently kept on planning and organizing the trip in his very special fabulous and perfect way, so that in the end everything turned out just fine.

On 11 September 2008, about 20 Cobweb musicians arrived in Munich and the adventure began. The hotel, run by the Gross family, in a small village near Dachau was not too bad, although some of you suffered a little bit from the busy church bells reminding everyone four times an hour of their existence. It was also a challenge to ferry everyone around in time for the rehearsals that took place in Dachau. The celli were provided again by a violinmaker from Munich. I unfortunately couldn't play having had surgery the week before, but my children helped out; this time Nikolai supported the cello section and enjoyed it very much as well as Svenja and Antonia playing violin. Some local musicians joined the orchestra, too, and all of you performed brilliantly in the main local Baroque church St. Jakob in the old center of Dachau playing probably the fastest Mozart (Symphony No. 40) ever and many other fantastic pieces. Jan, a young, very friendly and helpful percussionist, seized the opportunity and played classical music with an orchestra for the first time. On Sunday the orchestra had invited everyone in Dachau for a study day on Mahler's First symphony and many came to join in. As far as I recall everyone had lots of fun during these days and nights.

How everyone came back to Dachau in 2010

This time Priscilla Crumrine took over from Andrew with the organization of the trip and did a wonderful job. She speaks German very well, which helps a lot with communication. A new hotel, Hotel Hoerger, was found up North from Dachau, where the rehearsals could also took place, so that the daily commute to Dachau would no longer be necessary. It was a "Bio-Hotel" with many special features, among them rooms with a "built-in sauna" aka wooden cedar panels. The heat wave had just reached its peak, when you arrived on 14 July 2010. It proved to be a challenge for everyone and many secretly or openly wished they had booked rooms in an ordinary hotel with air-conditioning. It didn't help that 13 suitcases, some containing precious instruments, had been delayed on their way to Munich airport and would not appear until the next day or even later.

However, after everyone had been happily united with their belongings we were busy preparing the concert on Saturday in a Lutheran church, the Gnadenkirche, in Dachau. The programme was again wonderfully chosen and prepared by Andy, Beethoven's *"Pathetique" Ouverture*, Mozart's Alleluia from *Exsultate Jubilate* (with soloist), Helen Pyburn's *Blow the Wind Southerly*, Mozart's *Horn Concerto No.3* (with Sue Baker as soloist), Delius's Prelude from "Irmelin", Andy Jackson's The White Church (with soloist) and Schubert's *Symphony No. 5*. The singer was a beautiful young girl from Munich with an amazing voice, who enjoyed her parts as well as we all enjoyed listening to her. A heavy thunderstorm prevented many interested people from attending the concert, but the brave ones who came nevertheless, were thrilled. Before the concert some visited the Concentration Camp Memorial Site in Dachau. On Sunday there was again a study day in Dachau – Brahms' Symphony No.4 - with local musicians; this time even a guest conductor showed up and was happy to have such a patient orchestra in front of him. We all had a wonderful time together during those very hot summer days in the countryside. Some even made the long journey from the hotel all the way to Munich and enjoyed discovering the "biggest village" in Germany.

How everyone came back again in 2012

This time Priscilla rose to the challenge of being a mother of young Ryan and organizing the third trip to Dachau at the same time and she managed very well, with the help of husband Shane. Choosing the Youth Hostel in Dachau (Jugendgaestehaus Dachau) as new accommodation added to the challenge, because the arrangement of the rooms, every single meal, the rehearsal programme, in fact every tiny bit had to be discussed in advance with the team of the

Youth Hostel. As it turned out, when around 25 Cobwebbers arrived in Dachau on 22 August 2012, it was impossible to rearrange anything according to some new changes in the programme, the rules being unusually strict in the hostel. However, regarding the location – near the old town centre of Dachau, near the train station, including a nearly perfect rehearsal room – it was the best choice we had made in all those years. And the garden was just a perfect playground for the two lovely toddlers, who entertained their parents and the orchestra during the four days.

After the rehearsals and some chamber music many went to a local pub on the first night and had lots of fun. The second night was even better: the owner of a Mexican restaurant, being asked in advance whether he would allow them to make live music, happily approved of the idea and so many Cobwebbers played English, Scottish, Hungarian folk music with guitars, violins and the Northumbrian pipes. It was cool, Antonia said afterwards, which is the biggest compliment you could get from a teenager in Germany. The audience in the restaurant was puzzled, but seemed to like it.

The concert took place again in the Gnadenkirche and there was a notable audience this time, listening to fantastic music by Baines, Haydn, Hobbs (*The Alnwick Suite for Northumbrian Pipes and Orchestra*), Andy Jackson's *Jubilation*, Handel and Mozart. The Pipes sounded great and miraculously we were all in tune in the concert! Jan, the percussionist, joined us again for the concert and played brilliantly. This year there was no study day in the programme because of the summer holidays – almost everybody in Dachau leaves the town in August. Instead we wanted to perform an open-air concert on the most beautiful square of Dachau in front of the Baroque church in the old town center. Well, on that very day it turned out to be rather the scenery for a science-fiction movie: the night before four huge escalators wrapped in white plastic foil had been put down on that very square. They would be installed the next day, actually right after our short performance, into the department store next to the square. It was a very strange sight. The company deliberately and carefully had "forgotten" to notify anybody, not even the city council, in order to avoid any discussions. However, we played nevertheless, ignored the enormous white packages, dealt with the upcoming wind as well, and surprised the churchgoers and tourists with excellent music. I guess it was the weirdest "concert hall" an orchestra ever performed in! Only the most patient conductor in the world and the most relaxed and professional orchestra could deal with these circumstances. Andy and Cobweb Orchestra, we salute you!

How everyone will come back in the years to come

I dearly hope that looking back at these three memorable trips to Bavaria and Dachau there is still a longing in the Cobweb orchestra to find out how a trip without heat waves, thunderstorms, lost suitcases and monstrous escalators framing the orchestra, might feel. I am sure that having eventually found out the best accommodation, restaurant, and church there can't be too many problems anymore and anyway, we are such a good team – I know we would manage everything within seconds! In Dachau many people keep asking me when you'll be back – we are waiting for you all and hope you'll come back many times.

How can one distil the essence of the overseas trip? It is a cocktail of the chance to focus on one's music for a full week and lift personal playing standards by several notches; to have the time to really get to know fellow Cobwebbers better than a 15 minute coffee-break will permit; to enjoy the extraordinary sense of harmony that sharing such an experience brings and have all that under the umbrella of the stimulus that a trip to Tuscany / Hungary / Bavaria / brings.

But Harmony, in all its senses, would be the one most appropriate word to sum it all up.

9. Moving Forward

Reading through the newsletters produced in the 1990s, one forms the distinct impression of a new and pioneering organisation springing into life and operating on an informal basis with a home-grown newsletter, then a rather smarter one (sponsored by Marks and Spencer) then, in an attempt to look really professional, sharing a newsletter produced in collaboration with Northern Sinfonia and the Sage, and then, after going independent, creating our own even more sophisticated product with the help of the computer and home grown expertise.

There is also an apparent search for an identity as we grew at a breakneck pace rather like an adolescent in search of their true place in life and their relationship with the "significant others" around them. We described ourselves in the early days (1997-2002) as "the amateur orchestra with regular professional training". From 1997-2001 we were an "outreach project sponsored by Marks and Spencer," "a community orchestra for players of all ages and abilities" and from 2002-6 "Cobwebs - a special relationship with the Northern Sinfonia." From December 2006, as we moved towards independence, the "new look" newsletter was renamed "Don't lose the Thread".

So what had Cobwebs achieved over its first ten years? What did it stand for and what did it wish to carry forward? Could it survive in its present form or was it destined to change and turn into something much more conventional as it moved out of its pioneering days? Would interest peter out as players brushed up their skills, gained confidence and moved on into regular orchestras? Would the sheer size and complexity of the creature Andy had inspired overwhelm him? Would he lose his own enthusiasm for the project? All these possibilities seem preposterous looking back, but they must have been a real possibility at the time.

Speaking at the Cobwebs' tenth birthday party in Hexham, Andy, who had obviously done his homework, produced some impressive statistics. Over that time there had been nearly 900 rehearsals, involving around 14,700 attendances. There had been 86 study days, attracting 3,424 attendances, 132 concerts in 71 venues, including London and Tuscany, with around 5,500 musicians playing to audiences totalling 15,000 plus. This all added up to over a thousand events in over a hundred venues with nearly 24,000 "player bums on seats" as Andy described them.

From its initial role as an outreach project of the Northern Sinfonia, after the opening of the Sage, Cobwebs had come under the umbrella of their Learning and Participation Department. There were now issues on both sides of this partnership which made it preferable for the Cobwebs to move towards independence. Among these, the huge growth of the organisation over ten years meant that a great many tasks fell on Andy's shoulders - not only the artistic direction of the orchestra, (the leading of one group plus the oversight and support of all the others plus direction of most concerts, and devising of the weekend workshops), but also the burden of the administrative work went alongside all this activity, including finance, publicity and liaison with the Sage. The time needed to do all this far outstretched the limits of his half-time contract.

Certain aspects of Cobweb activity, such as the foreign trips and the Cabaret group already fell outside the administrative structure of the Sage and several activities had been organised by members of the orchestra, proving that there was both capacity and a willingness to run such events ourselves. So although the prospect of full independence could have appeared daunting, there seemed to be every prospect of being able to call on the skills and experience of members to help shoulder the workload. The Sage also offered continuing support during the transitional period, which allowed time for a full consultation with the membership and for a Working Party to consider the best way forward in terms of organisational structure.

An open meeting was held on October 28th 2006 at the Sage, where initial consultation took place as to what people valued about Cobwebs and where they wanted it to go. Comments ranged from "playing as an enjoyable activity, not competitive, choice of where and when to play, variety of repertoire, supporting beginners" to "important to conserve what is good as well as move to the new." Above all, a definite and firmly held principle, that of Open Access was confirmed. Inevitably, the practical day-to-day issues of funding and organisation also had to be discussed and valuable support was offered in all these areas by a Making Music representative, Robin Osterley, now Chief Executive of the organisation. Robin has kindly taken time to recall the meeting from his perspective:

Credit: Alex Rumford

"I well remember when I went, at Andy Jackson's request, trekking up to the Sage to a meeting of the Cobweb Orchestra about that least fascinating of topics, charitable governance (it was at that stage moving out from under the wing of the Sage Gateshead and Northern Sinfonia). Usually such a dry and uncreative subject is greeted with an understandable lack of enthusiasm, but I was very struck by the large numbers of people present and by their keenness and willingness to engage. This was a real measure of the democratic nature of Cobweb, and the fact that its members were so keen to see its next phase handled correctly and carefully was really good to witness. Andy had clearly built a real family of players and participants who wanted nothing but the best for the orchestra and who really impressed me with their commitment and open-mindedness. Cobweb has since become Making Music's largest member in terms of participants, and it is just wonderful to see how they have gone from strength to strength since their independence. All hail to Andy and his team!"

Katherine Zeserson from the Sage also assured members that they were keen for links with them to continue, as has been borne out by the setting up of the Sage Cobweb group which meets on Wednesday afternoons, the quarterly open workshops, and our sessions under the baton of the Sage's General Manager, Anthony Sargent.

To enable further consultation across the whole association and not just among those who were able to attend meetings, comments and suggestions were encouraged under headings such as ethos, structure, roles or funding, and Lee Fairlie offered to collate them. (Lee had been a lynchpin in the setting up of Cobwebs, and an enormous support through the progress towards independence. She was also the Chair of Cobfriends who stepped in during the transitional period, allowing their bank account to be used to deal with orchestra monies between the time the orchestra went independent and its beginning to trade as a registered charity and company.)

The Working Party also consulted widely over about six months as to the best constitution to adopt and finally decided that the most appropriate would be that of a charitable company limited by guarantee. A further meeting was held in January of 2008 to discuss the recommendations and also to consider membership and fees. A final vote was taken at a meeting in February 2008 at the Lamplight Arts Centre in Stanley, County Durham, appropriately, since it was at the invitation of Martin Weston, then Arts Officer for Derwentside, that the very first course was set up back in 1995.

Finally at a meeting in April 2007, trustees were elected to the board, and Cobwebs had achieved its independence.

Although the amount of consultation may seem excessive, the working party - then the trustees - could be sure that they had taken the membership of Cobwebs with them and ensured co-operation, support and a continuing group of very happy people. The three groups which existed prior to independence soon doubled to six with the Middlesbrough group starting in late 2007, and the York and Dalston groups in 2008, to be followed by the Sage group, and the newest group, in Spennymoor in 2010. New spin-off groups such as Composers and Arrangers sprang up, and existing specialist ensembles such as the Baroque Group went from strength to strength. The trustees set up a series of sub-committees, each dealing with a special aspect of the administrative load. Liz Carlile, who had taken over as librarian from Lee, was appointed part-time Administrator during the transition period, taking over from Susanna Wolfe of the Sage. Liz went on to do a splendid job behind the scenes, and making friends with everyone, and doubtless putting in many more hours than her allotted time.

At the time of writing the Role of Events Organiser is held by Sue Baker, French Horn player with the Consett Cobweb group. Sue combines organisational skills beyond compare in the planning of events, sending out regular newsletters, and answering queries with an amazing ability to produce vast amounts of delicious food, (but just the right amount) for our weekend workshops and fund-raising events.

The fears for the future voiced at the beginning of the process proved unfounded. Writing on the first year in a 2008 newsletter Howard Rocke, Chair of the Trustees, reflected that questions asked such as "would we be able to maintain a broad range of activities?" "Will open access be maintained?" "Would such a venture be financially viable?" could all be confidently answered "Yes!" At the first AGM in 2008 he reported that not only had activities continued as before but that several new departures were able to go ahead. He re-affirmed that "the people who make up Cobwebs are its bedrock."

Finances have sometimes given cause for concern, such as when Her Majesty's Revenue and Customs enforced limits on the Gift Aid we could claim. Also it was decided in the summer of 2011 that the cost of printing tickets for concerts was not retrieved in takings so the answer was to make concerts free and ask for donations, a plan which has proved most successful. The mere hint that trouble was brewing has always resulted in new ideas for fund-raising or a willing consent to the raising of fees. Almost as soon as independence was achieved, a huge auction was organised, and the second AGM was accompanied by a quiz and various other activities which not only lightened the atmosphere but also provided much needed cash. Other fund-raising ventures have included book sales, jam-making, knitted scarves, and two particularly effective initiatives by Cobweb members in Durham and Dalston.

After Cobwebs went independent more thought had to be given to fund-raising activities and one of these was the Cobweb Cookbook. This consists of recipes contributed by members and often sampled at Cobweb 'bring-and-share' meals. It was skilfully and attractively put together by Joan Murray, a viola player with the Consett group, who happens to work in corporate communications. The book was launched, appropriately, at a "Cookbook and Bites of Beethoven afternoon" in June 2010, where Cobwebs' two most popular activities were enjoyed to the full.

And then there is the Cobweb gear! Yes, the Cobweb Orchestra has its distinctive rugby shirt, hoodie or tee-shirt with the tasteful Cobweb bass clef design, also part of Joan's handiwork, a project organised by the Peter, Ruth, Julie and the Dalston group. The tops have been a great success, though they haven't succeeded in replacing the original and much loved formal concert outfit of white tops black bottoms and snazzy waistcoats.

Most recently a 200 Club has been set up, currently a popular form of fund raising, with a regular donation and a monthly draw.

The Cobweb Orchestra has successfully negotiated one major change in its structure over the course of its eighteen years existence. Like all groups which grow from small, pioneering beginnings, it has had to adapt to changes both within, largely that of huge growth, and also changes in the outside environment, ranging from the creation of Sage Gateshead and individuals' conditions of service, to the general economic environment in which we operate. Change however, is also a continuum, as we have seen numbers of groups increase and individual membership grow to well over one thousand people. There will certainly be change still to come, and what the future holds of course remains unknown, though some elements are predictable. We have seen changes in leadership in some groups and this will continue. Like all sensitive and responsive bodies, we have survived intact by ensuring that what goes on at the grass roots continues almost unaffected by changes in management. Groups have continued to meet, and the views and suggestions of members continue to be taken on board and respected. This sensitivity to the 'way the wind is blowing' whether openly expressed or not, runs all the way through our activities, from the reactions of players in a group session or a concert ('Help, I can't play this' 'I/we don't like this piece', or even voting with our feet) to the planning of major events and the very process of changing our organisational structure. As long as this awareness is embraced by future leaders there can be no doubt that the ethos of Cobwebs will be maintained. It will be sustained by the continuing desire of members in the community to take part in Cobwebs' unique style of music making.

10. Spin Offs: From the Intended to the totally Unexpected

"Speaking personally, I can now make my own pasta." (Sheila Blackwell after a Tuscany Residential.)

In addition to the on-going programme of regular weekly meetings, weekend workshops, special events and residentials, there are a number of outcomes both planned and unexpected which add to the rich tapestry which is the life of the Cobweb Orchestra.

Recordings

The first CD the Cobwebs ventured to record, known appropriately as "First Spin" was in March 1999. Despite lengthy preparation time, just like any good meal, it lasted all of 22 minutes. It includes two works by Andy Jackson, his *Twenty Year Kiss* and *Spennyopolis* (see Special Events, Chapter 5). Also on the recording are Vaughan Williams' setting of *Greensleeves*, and a piece for clarinet and orchestra by Rossini. Tracy Reed, the clarinet soloist on that occasion, wrote:
"My first solo with Cobwebs was in 1999. One Thursday night at Annfield Plain Library Andy handed me the music for Rossini's *Variations for Clarinet and Small Orchestra*. It quickly became known as Variations for Small Clarinettist! It was recorded in Durham Town Hall in March 1999. Andy asked me if I would like to play it again in Dachau in Summer 2012. I tried to play it more quickly this time, so I could get through more notes without taking a breath, but it reminded me how much the orchestra had improved since we first played it." She had written in the notes on the cover of the CD: "Rossini's variations demonstrate the technical versatility of the clarinet, barely giving the player time to take a breath between each phrase." It is indeed a joyous and bubbly work played with great panache by Tracy who delighted orchestra and audience alike when she played it in Germany.

Tracy also had links with the *Twenty Year Kiss* which was played by Cobwebs at her wedding. Her friend, Lesley Wearmouth, wrote of this work:

"Penned by our muse and mentor, the *Twenty Year Kiss* is part of his opera *The Wyrd Sisters*. Throughout the work you can hear a frequently repeated theme which punctuates the piece, often with a crescendo. You will notice that the tune grows from a barely audible *pp* to a highly romantic *f* and then at the finish it fades away to silence. Written with the instructions to "play with feeling and great expression," the ensemble, in particular the strings, gets the opportunity to wring the hearts with a dramatic tune intended to bring a tear to the driest of eyes."

There were a few young musicians in the band which came together for this first recording. One of them, Christos Worsley, son of Katherine, wrote:

"I came in, I'm sure like many other people, not knowing what the end of the day's result would be. I also, like many other people, was recording for the first time. I sat down and looked around me. I felt like the only nervous person there. I, or we, got through the first piece successfully, and I found out that my doubt was false, and that made me slightly more confident. The next piece went by and we quenched our thirst. Then the next piece, followed by another break. I was tired, and now and then would miss my cue due to daydreaming. However, I survived and we ended just in time before I collapsed. Everyone was congratulating each other and talking about how they thought they had played."

But he need not have worried, for Jean Ord also remembered: "Well, I have to admit to being a wee bit nervous …." Later she observes "Our able conductor and recording engineers made us sound professional in a short space of time, or so it seemed…."

The second CD, Spin Off, was recorded at the Stanwix Arts Theatre in Carlisle in July 2002, included a Cobwebs favourite of the time, Andy's arrangement of Purcell's music for *Abdelazar, or The Moor's Revenge*. An extraordinarily contorted plot by Mrs. Aphra Behn, (often narrated by Liz Carlile, at various times Administrator and Librarian, and at all times friend and general factotum to all). At concert performances, the work yields only one well-known and often played tune, the Rondo, which became the theme for Britten's *Young Person's Guide to the Orchestra*. On this occasion Cobwebs gave an airing to the other eight movements in the Suite. This was followed by a Mozart piano concerto played by Stephanie Cant, and arranged by her to accommodate, in the usual Cobweb fashion, instruments which do not actually figure in Mozart's score.

Finally, a first, the Potter *Duo Concertant for violin, piano and orchestra*, mentioned elsewhere. Cip Potter gave the first London performance of several Mozart and Beethoven concertos arranging and embellishing them to suit the resources available - a man after Cobwebs hearts! Stephanie and Andy duly repaid the compliment, editing the work to remove some "florid and unnecessary pianistic extravagances", but fitting in well with "the Cobweb Orchestra's unique repertoire of imaginatively reconditioned works."

This was followed up in Summer 2003 by the Cobweb Collection vol.1 (sadly not followed up by vols. 2, 3 or 4), in which all the works on offer were either composed or arranged, and all were conducted by, Cobweb members. These included a beautiful setting of *Full Fathom Five thy Father Lies* by Derek Hobbs, Stephanie Cant's *Italian Serenade* and *Spider* by John Hawkes.

"The first piece I wrote specifically for the Cobwebs was *Spider* in 2002. The name really has no significance beyond the obvious Cobweb connection, yet at rehearsals I have heard many an attempt to derive some sort of story from the music! In the early days of Cobwebs there always seemed to be a shortage of strings and in *Spider* I used a "sweep" technique to bring players in when 'pointed at', effectively turning each player into a separate line and hopefully making the strings sound more numerous than they actually were. A word of warning here to would-be composers: any slightly unconventional notation is likely to be regarded with extreme suspicion and will necessitate hours of repeated explanation! However, to be fair, the piece has been aired by the Cobwebs on quite a number of occasions, and was even recorded at Monkwearmouth School in July 2003.(The CD has an amusing picture of the *ad hoc* percussion section at work on the cover.)"

Next came recordings of the *Gospel Requiem*,(described more fully in Chapter 5,) both the full scale version with over 200 performers, and a smaller scale 'touring' version with just six instruments accompanying a smaller choir.

Also in 2007, came an event which "someone" described as "a real first, a Cobweb CD that sounds wonderful!" The main work was the much-loved César *Franck Symphony in D Minor*, which the orchestra worked hard to do justice to. Preceding this, a small ensemble played the lovely *Siegfried Idyll* of Wagner, and then the *Hawkrigg Idyll*, composed by Andy Jackson for two members of the orchestra.

Just as Richard Wagner composed the *Siegfried Idyll* to be played outside his wife's bedroom door on the morning of her birthday in 1870, so the *Hawkrigg Idyll* was commissioned by Brian Tanner (double bass) for the 60th birthday of his wife Ruth (cello) in May 2007. She, like Cosima, was woken by the opening melody played by a group of friends at the bottom of the stairs, some who had come a considerable way to be there for 8am. Ruth found that words could not express her surprise and delight at this amazingly romantic gesture, though one friendly player said that *she* would not have wanted to emerge in her nightclothes to meet friends knowing how *she* looked first thing in the morning! This was indeed a major spin-off. There are not many people nowadays who have their own local composer at hand to write birthday odes on demand.

More recent CDs have included two under the baton of Anthony Sargent, the Mozart *Requiem* and Bizet's *Symphony in C*. See Chapter 6 for Anthony's comments on these.

CDs were the obvious "spin-offs", but there have been others both musical and completely incidental, like the making of many warm friendships and even deeper relationships, one such being the marriage of two Cobweb members, Sarah and Philip, and the ensuing arrival of two little boys, Matthew and Ben, who have been visitors to Cobweb sessions since their earliest days.

In 1999, Richard Alty wrote in the newsletter about an unexpected and valuable side-effect of playing with Cobwebs:

"There isn't much these days that teenagers are prepared to be seen doing with their parents. Music is one activity in which parents and children can participate together, sharing as equals the fulfilment and exhilaration of a good performance, or the disappointment when things don't go so well. Sitting together under a common baton, striving for a common musical outcome and a common quality of playing is an experience which is a privilege to share.

The way Cobwebs operates is particularly conducive to providing this shared experience across the generations. The Cobweb orchestra has always welcomed people of all ages and, particularly at the larger events, the spread of ages working in harmony is always a notable feature. Because it is open to people with a wide range of ability there is always generous support, help and encouragement offered to anyone who comes along. That was the main reason why I survived my first experience of playing in an orchestra in 1997 and have continued to enjoy playing, learning and progressing since. My son, Mark, joined this March (1999) and it has been good to see him being offered the same support. As we prepared for and recorded the CD together, we enjoyed discussing our favourite - and least favourite - parts of the pieces. We have shared some laughs when we recognised quotations from our parts in some of the most unlikely pieces of music we have heard since. Although we play different instruments, we even played the same part in one piece, so there was a check on whether I was practising enough as well as vice versa!

Whether this harmony has been musically as well as personally valuable people will have to judge from the CD!"

Sheila Blackwell again.

"For many people music is not only a joy but an escape from one's daily problems of health or otherwise - the music just "takes over." The orchestra has produced the most huge amount of fun over the years, many zany events like the Health and Safety Orchestra, (a Sunday morning extravaganza at Sedbergh), Flash mob orchestras in Newcastle market and the Bus station to name just three."

The Cobweb Orchestra Instrument Bank

Not content with taking people on with their current instruments, it was realised that sometimes people would have lost or sold their original instruments or that they would perhaps like to try another. The instrument bank therefore came into being, initially with just a few donated or (perish the thought) discarded instruments. In 2008 the bank was augmented by several instruments from the old Cumbria County music service.

Andrew Forsyth, the Custodian of the bank, wrote in a recent newsletter:

"This is one of the happier banking stories of recent years and involves the growing number of instruments that the orchestra has acquired over the years that are available, completely free of charge, lien or interest, to our widening community of players". (It is amazing to hear that the exact number now stands at 56 - what a good job that he has a large barn available!)

Our wish is that these should be available to anyone who fancies trying a new instrument or wants to re-kindle lost skills in that inimitable Cobweb fashion. Some instruments, like the oboe, horns and double bass are in constant demand and so regular turnover is important. As with any library, and especially a music one, keeping track of them is not easy, particularly when they are sometimes passed from one player to another without a trip "home" first, but it is usually quite easy to find a Cumbrian member who will be passing close-ish to Andrew in Weasdale, and the value of having this resource is tremendous, particularly in view of the amazing number of people who seem to want to try a new instrument, of which more anon.

Julie Ratcliffe wrote:

"I'm but one of many who have changed instrument thanks to the bank. As bank administrator, I've watched, amongst others, violinists try horns, trumpets and tubas and flautists sample trombones and cellos. Some will decide it's not for them, while others will take to their new instrument like a duck to water. Whatever the outcome, few would have even attempted the transition without the opportunity to borrow the new instrument – not many can shell out several hundreds if not thousands of pounds on a whim."

Cobfriends

The Cobfriends group was set up in 2003, partly to ensure that the orchestra had its own bank account at a time before we were independent. It also served a very valuable purpose in tiding us over between our former arrangement with North Music Trust and our gaining independent status. It uses funds from tea and coffee money and from small donations and fundraising activities to provide secondary but much appreciated support to members, such as flowers or gifts to those who may fall ill, or have a baby, or leave, or to provide flowers or gifts for guest artists. It has also helped with the provision of items of equipment such as a conductor's podium, a marquee, or providing matched funding which enabled the purchase of a piece of music still in copyright. Perhaps its most helpful function is to make bursaries available for those who may have difficulty paying either fees for individual events or a membership fee for the year, a very practical way to ensure that the open access principle really does mean just that. Applications are handled confidentially and hopefully mean that no-one who would like to is prevented from making music with the Cobweb orchestra.

Cobweb meets Academia

There are at least three occasions on which the Cobweb orchestra has assisted in academic research studies. The first was in 2003 and was a project organised jointly by the Universities of Newcastle and Durham with the Centre for Life under the banner of the Policy, Ethics and Life Sciences Research Institute. It was called Memory and Forgetting, and was intended to 'develop partnerships between visual arts and neuroscientists to explore different dimensions of memory and forgetting.' The Cobweb orchestra, represented by the Music by Heart group, presented a 'collaboration sci-art event' called Music in Mind.

Then in 2007 a small group took part in 'Swing Cycle', an exercise in setting language acquisition research to music. It was organised by Martha Young-Scholten from the Linguistics Department of Newcastle University under the Aim Higher programme, and also involved two Tyneside schools. Andy wrote a piece of music drawn from folk lullabies and environmental sounds, combining music and 'linguistic games'. The Cobweb participants were often a little bewildered by the process, but as ever, co-operative, and as Andy put it 'willing to do the oddest things with cheerful good grace.'

Most recently, in April 2013, Barbara Griffin presented a paper entitled 'An Open Access Orchestra; Social Capital and Reduced Public Spending' at the BSA 'Engaging in Sociology' conference in the Connaught Rooms in London, as part of the Culture, Media and Sport programme. The paper was based on six participatory appraisals collated from the Cobweb Orchestra's 2012 Cultural Olympiad 'Celebrating Four Centuries of English Music' project funded by the Arts Council England and the Lottery Fund.

In her presentation, Barbara explored how the private problems of financing additional Cobweb events is also a public issue, and how recent government cuts to the Arts and Culture budgets affects community based organisations such as ours. The value that members place on Cobwebs activity exemplifies building social capital and networks in the community. She went on to discuss the limitations placed on participation by financial considerations, and her argument was that additional financial support to an orchestra like Cobwebs can go towards broadening the membership base to a wider range of people beyond the educated middle classes.

Cobwebs Hits the Headlines…

…Or at least the Arts section of the Guardian. Charlotte Higgins is the chief arts writer for the paper and describes herself as 'amateur violinist and classicist', in that order! In 2009, she began to explore the vast range of amateur music groups active across the country, of which she noted that there were around 11,220 identified in a government report. She began to visit some of these groups, ('duets in Glasgow, trios in Edinburgh, quartets in London') and towards the end of the year she bravely made her way to Consett with her violin, to take part in an evening with the Cobweb orchestra group which meets there. Having quizzed the two Cobweb members who fetched her from Durham station to Consett continually during the car ride, she spoke to members during the break and then in the pub afterwards. As a result of this we gained a three page article and several pictures in the 19th January 2010 edition, and lots of very welcome publicity.

Charlotte obviously enjoyed her time with us, and wrote thoughtfully about the "slur" of amateurism and how in the last century before the advent of recorded music "if you wanted to get to know a piece of music, you might well have to play it yourself." Towards the end of her article she quotes Andy: 'Why is it that in our culture doing something extremely complex –like playing a musical instrument- only quite well isn't really valued? Surely there's something wrong with that?' An interesting point to ponder!

Awards

To most members of Cobwebs these come in the "unexpected" category, but in fact someone must have taken the trouble to make the applications and to them we must be grateful for the prestige and the publicity they bring with them. They also, in a sense, lend credibility to the value of what we do in the face of those who sometimes "look down their noses" at our efforts.

2011 was the "Annus Mirabilis" for Cobweb awards. We received two national awards and were shortlisted for a third, in recognition of our creative approach to innovation and inclusivity in the world of amateur music making.

The EPIC award from Voluntary Arts England was designed to recognise excellence among the fifty thousand voluntary arts organisations across the country. We won First Prize in the Innovation category for the Undercover Orchestra Bolero - a flash mob rendition of Ravel's Bolero at Eldon Square Bus Station in Newcastle. The event was filmed and viewed on YouTube more than 30,000 times in its first week alone, and as Chrissie reports in Chapter 5, has now passed the half a million mark! Andy and trustee Elizabeth Beer received the award at a reception in the House of Lords in January 2011.

Photo © Voluntary Arts England/Jacky Chapman

We also struck it lucky in the Music in the Community award which came from Gramophone Magazine in association with Making Music and the Times newspaper. The appealing aspect of this award was that the final judgement was made by public vote in the Times. The award was received by Andy and Catherine Shackell, then the Cobweb Administrator, at a reception in the Dorchester Hotel on 6th October 2011.

Andy said that the philosophy of the orchestra was that it "focuses on the way in which an orchestra benefits its local community looking at the philosophy of inclusivity, the opportunities it provides and the enrichment and values it offers. The Cobweb orchestra with its all-comers policy (no auditions, no-one turned away, music varied in style and level of difficulty, with bursaries for those who may find it difficult to finance their playing) has as its overarching aim the desire to enable as many people as possible to share in the joy of live music."

An Individual Award

Cobwebs is a very egalitarian orchestra and always delights in the good playing of its members, but occasionally someone in the orchestra achieves something very special that we all take pride and delight in. One such was when Michael Cave won the Geoffrey Gilbert Adult Amateur competition organised by the British Flute Society. Mike, a busy cardiologist by profession, plays with the Consett group, and now with several other orchestras. He has always delighted the group with the quality of his flute playing and it was great that his talent and dedication was recognised elsewhere.

The Ravenstonedale Prom

Sometimes, and quite often in fact, a one–off event which the orchestra takes on turns out to be so popular that it becomes a regular commitment. At one time Music by the Lake in Keswick was one of these but this has since been eclipsed, despite the best efforts of the weather, by the Ravenstonedale Prom. Sheila fills in the background and sets the scene.

"A sunlit evening in this Yorkshire Dales village, a gentle stream running beside the garden of the Black Swan Hotel to the accompaniment of beautiful music, the audience lounging on rugs with their picnics and drinks, enjoying an idyllic evening while a fine singer's voice soars over the orchestra." These were the thoughts that passed through the mind of Richard Best when he set up the first Ravenstonedale Prom.

In reality, there was always a worry over the weather, so a marquee was borrowed from the Sedbergh Town Band, the instruments being too precious to be ruined in a sudden squall. That sudden squall became a reality as we erected the big tent. The wind howled and the rain lashed down. However, the day of the Big Event dawned fair and glorious, hot sun emerging as a large orchestra gathered for an afternoon of rehearsing, and we included a few children in musical games while the audience enjoyed an afternoon of music and their picnics. It was a great triumph, and so it was decided to repeat the Prom the following year, with our own "lit up" marquee this time. We had an even larger orchestra including 5 double basses - another great success.

The following year Richard made a rostrum which was ceremonially set in place for Andy to conduct from, only to find that his head was over the edge of the marquee, we could only see his body and he couldn't see us - so it was abandoned for that event.

This was the year the Dales Midge population had gathered their friends and relations and descended on us all in a large cloud as the lights came on in the marquee and we started to play. String players' bows waved furiously at the hordes of bugs, our conductor, Andy's arms became a windmill, those not playing smacked their heads and chests and the audience wriggled on their rugs – and some ran into the pub! Poor Britannia could hardly open her mouth to sing before being invaded by bugs.

So it was decided to abandon our outdoor idyll and move instead to the lovely St. Oswald's Church in the village which is perfect for music-making if a little cramped for a large band and a long way from the toilets in the pub! The next concert coincided with heavy rain and a Folk Festival in the garden where we had played previously. Mercifully the move to the Church saved us from the thick gloopy mud, and wearing wellingtons, whereas the "Folk" looked happy and unmoved by the lashing rain. Meanwhile in the Church we gave a lovely concert and made a reasonable amount of money for the Church as well as for our own funds.

With St. Cecilia gazing down on us from her stained glass window in this lovely church we gave our Jubilee Prom. Britannia, resplendent in full regalia gave us her all (no midges) with an orchestra of forty players. Because of the size of the orchestra it was necessary to move two very large pews, a major feat involving six strong persons, straps and a bogey, all executed with great precision. One of the highlights of the evening was conductor Peter Crompton playing a Shirley Bassey number on his trumpet. This was another concert to remember. They have all been really happy events both musically and socially, and a great way to raise funds for the local church and of course for the unique and fabulous Cobweb orchestra- long may it live!"

"Cobwebs Round the Side"

Not all events lead to successful spin-offs. One letter which had us chuckling was received by Andy after a concert in a village in south Durham.

"I popped into the Parish hall in Sedgefield yesterday morning, in connection with our Drama festival this week, to find the cleaning lady in a furious rage, with a piece of paper in her hand. On the paper was written the legend "Cobwebs round the side." Not knowing the name of the orchestra (all she knew was that the booking had been made in the name of a Mr. A. Jackson) she waved the paper in my face and uttered something like 'The cheeky b******s! This is the first time they've been here and they've got the nerve to complain about a few ****** cobwebs. Well, I've looked round the sides of the hall and I can't see any! The nerve of some people-and they seemed so nice when they came to look round!'

It took me a full five minutes to persuade the good lady that what she held in her hand was merely a helpful note directing the members who hadn't been to Sedgefield before to the appropriate entrance, and that "Cobwebs" was the name of the orchestra and in no way a criticism of the cleanliness of the Parish Hall! Once she had calmed down we were all able to have a good laugh and I was able to tell her that far from being unhappy with the venue, they would like to make a return visit" (but we never have, in fact, ever gone back!)

Inspiration for other Art Forms

Cobwebs can inspire us to creativity in other art forms too. Over the years, people have created art works which have adorned notelets and newsletters, and on one occasion, the Earswick 'Come and

Play' Haffner Day in 2008, David Jasper was moved to write what Cyril Fletcher would have called an 'odd ode' distilling the essence of the Cobweb experience.

Cobwebs

Did you ever play an instrument, then give up after a while?
Was practice an intrusion on the things that made you smile?
Has the dust begun to settle on your instrument's black case?
If you took it out to play it would your friends run off apace?
Well, I think I have the answer to your problem my dear friend,
A solution that will hopefully your low confidence mend.
You need to find a group of people who were once like you
And pick up where you left off, with a 'not-so-motley' crew!

I know you're feeling anxious and would like to start again
And now's the time to do it, now you have the time and when
You find that group of people, who were similarly shy,
Like them just bite the bullet and give it one more try.
There's a group that meets in Harelaw, another at Newbiggin
A third across at Tebay that will get your legs a-jiggin'.
A fourth one meets at Middlesbrough inside the Town Hall crypt
And the newest is at Earswick, York, according to my script.

They come under the strange title of The Cobweb Orchestra.
You should go and join them, for they'd welcome an extra.
They've players young and middle-aged and knocking on a bit
But what unites these lovely folk is music, food and wit.
They have professional players and amateurs alike.

One thing's for sure, you won't be told to go home "On your bike!"
I guarantee you'd be made welcome, probably get a hug
And within twenty minutes, you'd have the Cobweb bug.

They're a lovely set of people, fond of Mozart, Bach and Liszt,
Beethoven and Mahler and some others that I've missed.
They gather fairly frequently with instrument and stand,
Together with a shared tea, which is always very grand.
Go along and join them, just go in and say, "Oh, hello!"
Take your oboe or bassoon with you, your trombone or 'cello.
Once you've played the first few bars, you'll wonder, "Why did I worry?"
And go back the next time 'accelerando' (in a hurry!)

11. Finding the right instrument

Time for a Change

A surprising number of "Cobwebbers" turn out to have been players of other instruments who have changed since joining the orchestra for one reason or another. Sheila Ryan describes elsewhere (Chapter 2) how she graduated from flute down through the ranks of the recorder consort to her present instrument, the bassoon. Several other flute players changed because in the early days of Cobwebs there was often a great number of flautists in the group. In fact, most of the Consett French horn section is composed of those who originally played another instrument; Sue (oboe), Lee (flute) Helen (violin) and Julie Ratcliffe, another flute, who here describes how her horizons have extended even beyond Cobwebs.

A Tyrolean Idyll, and it's all down to Cobwebs…

"At first it seems a tenuous connection, but without our amazing organisation and its resources, I simply would never have been in Seefeld in the autumn of 2012.

Back in 2009 at an instrument swap session at our spring Sedbergh residential weekend, I had the temerity to mention to Lee Fairlie that I hankered after trying the horn. Branded the most difficult instrument in the orchestra to play, you might say I was setting my sights high, but having spent so many years sitting in front of the horn section, as a flute player, I'd been seduced by the sound. Also, I've reached that wonderful stage in life where a give-it-a-go attitude has taken over – after all, everything has a 'now or never' urgency to it once you reach middle age!

Under Lee's gentle but encouraging tutoring, I attempted to blow first a raspberry into the mouthpiece and then to get a note from the yards of brass tubing that is the double horn. I seemed to manage both (although heaven knows which notes I was getting) and that was it - I was hooked. However, as someone who doesn't like to give up on a project once started, I then spent some weeks pondering the consequences of this proposed adventure. The issues of pitching and transposing were the most daunting (and still are) but having thought about it throughout the ensuing months, in September I borrowed a horn from the Cobweb instrument bank.

I'm of the firm belief that a good teacher is required for most worthwhile things in life, if only to avoid developing bad habits which are subsequently impossible to reverse and, as chance would have it, and quite serendipitously, a horn teacher lives in the same village as me. I knew Pam slightly, and finding myself in her company at a bonfire night party, I took the plunge and enquired how she felt about taking on an adult beginner. "Great!" was her reply and my first lesson was organised for the following week.

That was in 2009 and, yes, pitching and transposing still cause problems, but under Pam's expert guidance and with Lee's continued encouragement (I call her my mentor) I now find I'm playing an instrument that I love. Does it suit my psyche and character more than the flute? That's probably for others to say, but what I do know is, learning to play the horn has opened up so many opportunities for me. Flute players abound, but horn players are slightly less numerous, and I now find I have opportunities to play with groups and orchestras that would have been unattainable in the past.

So often in life, it's the new people we meet through different activities who open doors for us. In the summer of 2012, Pam introduced me to the Scottish Vienna Horns (SVH), who, as the name indicates, are all aficionados of the Vienna single F horn, as most famously played by the Vienna Philharmonic.

SVH get together at regular intervals and play horn ensemble music in a variety of locations, including an autumn residential weekend in Austria. The repertoire is eclectic and includes arrangements of well-known symphonies for anything from eight horns upwards – if you've never heard a large group of horns playing together, make sure you do as it's a magical sound!

That's how I came to be in the Tyrol, playing fantastic music on a wonderful instrument. And so I'd say the link is anything but tenuous, because without the amazing Cobweb Orchestra and its invaluable instrument bank giving me the chance to 'have a go', I can safely say I would not have been in Seefeld that weekend.

The Cobweb Orchestra is a multifaceted organisation but, at its core, is its role as a facilitator, whether encouraging lapsed players to return to the music scene or beginners to join in and make music together with others; in coaching new conductors; or inspiring would-be composers and arrangers.

Long may this unrivalled organisation continue to offer to amateur musicians in the north of England, these unique, life enhancing-and indeed, life-changing opportunities."

A New Start

Hilda Sim relates both her arrival in the Cobwebs Spennymoor group, and her delight in discovering her true place in the orchestra!

"After an unfortunate time in Ireland, I returned to the UK to start a new life. I joined a community choir and enjoyed my first foray back into music since violin lessons at school.

Then I met an old friend I hadn't seen in decades. We were both in the school orchestra but she had continued with the oboe and now plays every week with the Dundee Symphony Orchestra. She was my inspiration. Would it be possible to start playing violin again after thirty-five years off? I started googling 'amateur orchestra north east' and the Cobweb Orchestra kept popping up. If I had tried to specify my ideal orchestra, this would have been it. There were no auditions and it was also open to beginners and those who hadn't played for a long time. I emailed Catherine Shackell and she sent me the newsletter. But I still wasn't quite ready.

In March 2011 I went to a charity concert by the Heavy Cavalry and Cambrai Band and their live performance cast a spell on me. This was my light bulb moment – the moment I knew I had to join a band somehow. Still nervous, I phoned Greg and Andy and asked if I could come along and listen. I was given a very warm welcome when I went to my first group rehearsal at Spennymoor. I wasn't intending to play; didn't even have an instrument. However as soon as I arrived, somebody (mentioning no names) thrust a violin into my hands and, ignoring my feeble protests, told me to "Sit down and play!"

I couldn't remember the names of the strings, G, D, A, E; had forgotten about positions and playing chords; could hardly remember which hand to hold the bow in. I looked at the music, a Beethoven symphony. The page was a black scrawl of too many notes, almost indecipherable compared to our choir music.

Playing that first time was terrifying: like being thrown out of an aeroplane and trying to remember how to use the parachute on the way down. I was mortified at how badly I played. On the way home I wondered whether I would dare return the following week. However I was already hooked.

Shortly after joining the orchestra I injured my arm - which was a stroke of luck as it gave me the excuse to put down the violin and pick up the trumpet instead. I had not really enjoyed playing violin at school but was given no choice of instrument and had persevered so as to be in the orchestra. I nursed an ambition to play a wind instrument. Was it my imagination that the wind section was having more fun? Or was it to do with sitting at the back of the class away from teacher?

I bought a trumpet twenty years ago but never got round to learning to play. It stayed trapped in its case, but something stopped me from getting rid of the brassy thing while it gathered dust and cluttered up the house like an accusation. I gave it a good clean (dusted off the cobwebs!) and practised at home until I could play almost an octave then 'came out' at a Cobwebs brass ensemble, my trumpet debut. I never dreamed I could join an orchestra so soon after beginning, but the Cobwebs ethos allowed me to play as a novice at the Spennymoor group. Without this, I don't think I would have ever been able to learn to play. Catch 22 – you can't join a band until you're good enough but you can't become good enough without joining a band. Cobwebs seems to be full of switchers who have learned a new instrument: cello to viola; flute to French horn; violin to trombone; trumpet to violin; and so on. What makes people prefer different instruments? Is there a personality type better suited to wind or strings, or is that just stereotyping?

As soon as I began to play the trumpet, I knew I was going to enjoy it. It was like taking off the wrong size of shoes, cramped and pinching, and putting on comfy old slippers. Playing trumpet with the full orchestra is a rollercoaster of excitement. When you blow, what note will emerge?

It can be frustrating when progress is slow. I often wonder how on earth I was able to learn the violin as a youngster: it seems so difficult now. But although challenging, it is not impossible. It is reassuring that some of the skill eventually starts to return. I do admire adults who start learning from scratch without previous experience of a musical instrument.

People in the orchestra are willing to give advice and support. My comrades have been encouraging and amazingly tolerant of my attempts to play. I enjoy being the least experienced player because there is less pressure. With Cobwebs, you are allowed to make mistakes.

Since I joined a year ago I've enjoyed abundant opportunities to participate, including weekly groups, weekend study days and residentials. The first event I took part in was a performance of Beethoven's 4th *Piano Concerto*. As a beginner, I was overwhelmed to be given the chance to accompany a professional pianist at the Sage. For me it was an extremely moving and memorable occasion.

Lots of work goes on behind the scenes, mostly voluntary, eg. organising events, taking care of sheet music, fund-raising, providing tea and biscuits, etc. Not forgetting a wealth of shared food, especially the cakes…

There is a great camaraderie when playing music together. You feel a common bond without having to share your life story or make scintillating conversation. Would it be too fanciful to say that conflicts could be resolved and wars averted if people would sit down together and play music?

I feel very lucky to be a member of the orchestra. It's addictive and it's exhilarating and has far exceeded my expectations."

The Secret Life of a Percussionist

Doug Dawson has gone from "Zero to Hero" of the orchestra with his cool approach to mastery of the percussion section, a role he only took up on his retirement.

"The qualifications you need to be a good percussionist are no doubt many and varied, but the most important are: enjoying moving lots of heavy equipment; the ability to count to at least 300 at a range of different speeds; a strong tendency to be an exhibitionist; and the ability not to get irritated when people suggest that a piccolo might be a better bet.

To give you an idea what it's like, allow me to describe one of the most demanding events I have played in so far – the dreaded Bishop Auckland Prom. Why dreaded? It was a big event involving serious pre-planning: it was outdoors in unpredictable weather; it drew a large audience; and it involved a huge number of relatively short pieces of music of bewildering variety. Consequently it called for many different percussion instruments, all of which had to be played by myself (there was no room on stage for anyone else).

The first requirement was to get hold of the parts in advance. This is essential for this sort of concert, if only to find out which instruments to bring. The wonderful Liz managed to get almost all the parts to me, and from this I worked out that I needed 3 timpani, a pedal bass drum, hi-hat cymbals, a ride cymbal, a triangle, and a snare drum, plus sticks and beaters, stool, two music stands, tuning keys, a tuner, clothes pegs,(to keep the music on the stands) and a mountain of heavy supporting metalwork. Even with all this paraphernalia, there were some parts I couldn't cover (Walton's *Crown Imperial*, for example, is written for four players). Then I had to go through working out changes of key for the timps, when to move between timps and drum kit, when to put down sticks and pick up beaters, and so on.

We knew that the first part of our afternoon rehearsal was indoors. Then we would move to the outdoor stage for a sound check and more rehearsal. Arrival for Barbara and me at Bishop Auckland College was encouraging, with a huge car park, easy access to the rehearsal space, and a whole hour to get set up. Then everything fell apart as the door was not unlocked until 15 minutes before the rehearsal and I was dead before I'd started. This is what I really hate! I was in a complete flap for the next hour, never being properly ready for anything, and, I have to confess, being in a seriously grouchy mood for which I profoundly apologise.

We moved on to the outdoor stage with the wonderfully welcome help of an army of carriers who transported my stuff over the field. Luckily we got the car close to the stage, and gradually we all squeezed into the very limited space. A stiff cold breeze blew through the gap in the canvas just behind the brass players and myself, and clothes pegs were much in evidence. As we rehearsed, roadies buzzed about with microphones, and the area in front of the stage was populated by an enthusiastic horde of teeny boppers waiting to catch sight of Joe McElderry, but they were suitably hushed by the stunning Min-Jin Kym playing Bruch and the lovely voice of Susan Robertson. Andy, our wonderful conductor, was calmness itself even when Joe decided to sing with a backing track rather than with the orchestra.

During the tea break I managed to completely retune my small timpani from scratch – one tuning screw had worked loose in transit and it sounded horrible. The concert itself went amazingly well despite the wind and the distractions of some of the teeny boppers. Special moments for me personally were: getting through the fiendishly difficult, and very prominent, snare drum part in *Pirates of the Caribbean* without too many mishaps; *Midsummer Night's Dream* (Mendelssohn wrote wonderful timp parts); and of course *Crown Imperial*, which is just a thrill from start to finish. Gradually, as we played, the wind died, the evening sun emerged, the audience became increasingly enthusiastic, and by the end we could have played yet more encores. Again helpers appeared to pile all the gear into the car, and we wearily but happily drove off into the night.

When I retired nine years ago, never having played any musical instrument, the very idea that I could ever play in an orchestra was unthinkable, so the whole experience is just the best thing ever! This is what the Cobweb organisation does – it picks you up and cheerfully carries you forward, inspired by players around you. A huge thank you to Pauline, to Andy, to my long-suffering wife Barbara (who got me into this in the first place), to Ian, Noel and Peter (our conductors at Tebay) and everyone in this wonderful Cobweb orchestra for all their encouragement. May it last for ever."

Over in the North East, (Doug plays in Cumbria) there was no percussionist until Pauline Holbrook, originally a flautist took up the challenge. Here in an excerpt from a newsletter article in 1999 she shows why the percussion section is sometimes referred to as the 'kitchen department.'

"Everyone, I soon discovered on joining, is welcome at Cobwebs, which is why there are sometimes five flute players and a similar number of clarinettists, so it is not uncommon for us to help out on second violin, or to fill in for a missing brass part.

On about my third rehearsal, with full attendance in the flute section and a concert in the offing, Andy looked in our direction and asked if any of us fancied trying the percussion part. As I was still sight-reading some of the flute music, what had I to lose? The first piece was over before I'd even worked out which movement we were on: the second contained gong, drum, cymbal and triangle, all of which had been borrowed for the evening by another member of the orchestra.

Next problem: how to practise for the concert. It's amazing what you can do with a pan lid, stainless steel goblet and a child's drum. The pitch isn't spot on, but it does help with the timing.

Five months after joining the Cobweb Orchestra my flute is no longer lonely in the dining room. It gets played most days and it is now kept company by a trio of drums and a cymbal which I have borrowed. I won't tell you what the family said when these appeared, but two of them are now learning the clarinet!"

Since writing this, Pauline has sadly had to give up percussion, and has sold her kit, but did take up the oboe. That, we guess, is another story!

Tracy Reed, has yet another, and cunning way to get a feeling for other instruments' perspectives in the orchestra. She plays those parts on her own family of clarinets, or in her words, she "pretends" to be other instruments. Here she describes some of the challenges and pitfalls involved, as well as the benefits of getting a new perspective on the orchestral scene.

"When the orchestra first started we were a small group and the clarinets would often be given the parts that were left over, even to try to play two parts at the same time. I think my first attempt at pretending was with an oboe part. An oboe part is in C but a clarinet is in B flat so everything has to move up a tone. If there is a C then I have to play a D, an A flat becomes a B flat and so on. A flute is in C like an oboe and I've pretended to be a flute too, but the music has so many ledger lines to count, and a clarinet playing that high doesn't sound as beautiful as a flute. More recently I started to pretend to be a bassoon. It took me a while to get used to playing in the bass clef. Now I had to play an octave lower than written, but still up a tone. If the music was very low sometimes I'd "run out" of notes at the bottom, so found I was jumping an octave and then back again - phew! I'd end up doing the intervals the wrong way round and would get the giggles. Brian on double bass asked "What pitch are you playing in?" and I don't think I really knew. So Santa solved that problem by delivering a bass clarinet which sounds an octave lower than a B flat clarinet. Mine goes down to a bottom C below middle C. That means it is also bigger. Why didn't I think of that? It's almost as big as I am, and I have to have a set of steps to sit on, but I love it.

You may also have seen me with a little E flat clarinet. I'm not playing it just because I've got small fingers; it's used to make those high shrill sounds that would be much more difficult on a B flat instrument. I usually warn people in front before I play it, but there are some fantastic solos. When we did Berlioz's *'Symphonie Fantastique'* I was the witch!

Clarinettists usually have a pair of instruments, one in A as well as one in B flat, to avoid scary key signatures. Conductors need to watch out for a change in instrument between movements to make time for a swap, or the poor clarinettists almost knock their teeth out. (That was before the Queen arrived ...) If you're a clarinettist you also have to make sure you are playing the correct instrument. I confess to once playing Stravinsky's symphonies of wind instrument on the wrong clarinet, but I don't think anyone noticed ... I also once joined half my B flat clarinet to half of my A clarinet. Whoops!

Bassoon parts and trombone parts are written in the tenor clef as well as the bass clef, which may appear tricky for a clarinet who only uses the treble clef, but here's the trick. Pretend it is the treble clef and don't transpose. Similarly if you are pretending to be a viola in the alto clef pretend it is a bass clef and don't transpose. Horn parts take me longer to work out. Up a fifth? Yikes! Do all horn players prefer accidentals to key signatures, or is it just Jeremy?

Pretending to be other instruments has made me really listen to the other players in the orchestra. If you play the first clarinet part, you need to listen to the first flute and first oboe as our melodies often go together. If I am a bassoonist, I listen to the cellos and double basses a lot more. Sitting in a different place in the orchestra is interesting too. I like sitting with the clarinets in the middle, right opposite the conductor. Isn't it harder when you play the violin or the cello and have to watch the conductor from the side? I like being on my 'high chair' with my bass because I can see everything. What do the conductor and the first violins always talk about? What are the oboists doing with their reeds? What do horn players do with their hands? Has the bass player noticed that a small child is approaching fast holding a drumstick?

When you are pretending to be other instruments you have to consider how they sit. A bassoon needs space next to their seat. Cellists want some space in front of them for their pieces of carpet. You really don't want to get on the wrong (I mean right) side of a piccolo. If you are a wind player, and you end up in the string section, watch out for the end of a bow in your head, and be polite and pick up their music scattered on the floor. They won't be used to getting spit all over their music!

Pretending to be different instruments has also made me more aware of the technicalities that players have to overcome. I didn't know that an oboe has three register keys. A clarinet only has one. How do string players know when to bow up or down? And do they really not know how to count? How can I possibly project sound like a trumpet? I understand now why people talk about tone colour. Pretending to be another instrument has helped me to learn more about orchestration. And as well as giving me a better understanding of all the instruments in the orchestra, pretending has given me an even greater respect for the musicians who play them. I like being part of the Cobweb family; we celebrate each other's achievement. *I'm not pretending about this.* The Cobweb orchestra is very special."

12. The Philosophy of Music-making – the Cobweb Way

One does not often stop to think about it, but the amazing institution which is the Cobweb Orchestra does not just happen by chance. A great deal of thought and planning went into the realisation of the project, and the philosophy on which it is based continues to inform the way activities are organised at every level. This applies from overall programme planning for the year down to the details of each and every weekly session across the region, and every workshop.

When Stephen Pettitt founded the New Tyneside orchestra in 1970 it was with the aim of "improving the standards of music-making on Tyneside." Whilst this is an entirely laudable and not uncommon aim for a local amateur orchestra, it is rather different from the ethos of Cobwebs. Though we always strive to produce as polished a performance as possible, the emphasis with us is on the performer, and also on the "here and now". Our music making is for the joy of playing and doing the best we can at the time. Indeed there are quite a few "Cobwebbers" who rarely if ever take part in our set-piece concerts, preferring the more informal setting of the weekly meeting. We also serve to inspire those who do wish to reach greater heights of perfection, by giving them a start, a "jumping – off point" and the confidence to move on into the wider world of music-making.

One of the phrases most often used to describe the Cobweb orchestra is that we are "open access." This inevitably means that we do not always hit the heights, but it offers the experience of playing in a group which can inspire one to greater endeavour, or just that wonderful feeling of being a part of the music, being "on the inside looking out" as one member described it, rather than just admiring the music from afar. In this way one learns so much more about the pieces we play, one hears more of the subtleties of the orchestration and the nuances of phrasing.

"We have often noticed that when a piece of music comes up on the radio that we have played in Cobwebs, we 'hear' it in quite a different way. We now understand better what makes that characteristic Sibelius sound (rumbling lower strings) or the boisterous sweeping string sound of Elgar. Even if we can't immediately place it, we know we've played it. (Now where was it?)"

Part of the freedom of open access is that one does not have to go every week. Since we do not always have our sights set on an 'end of term' concert, we are not confined to rehearsing two or three pieces exclusively for a long period. "Cobwebs play for the moment." This has the benefit of allowing us to cover a variety of music catering to the shape of the group which has assembled. When Sarah and Emma Gait were young they came along to several Cobweb events in Cumbria, including workshops and study days. They were talented young musicians who also played in the National Children's Orchestra and in an article in 2004 they drew some comparisons between the two orchestras:

"Cobwebs can't always produce such a high standard as the NCO, but it also means there is less pressure at Cobwebs about full accuracy, about which NCO is very emphatic. Because of this NCO chooses less demanding pieces. Conversely, Cobwebs chooses difficult but exciting music such as Shostakovich's *8th Symphony*, (in which we played <u>nearly</u> all the notes). It aims for a high standard without putting too much pressure on anyone.

One thing Cobwebs has taught us is to sight-read very well!"

There are other benefits too. For the beginner, the first experience of playing in an orchestra is daunting. The music just "flies past you" as Andy so aptly puts it. Gradually however, you learn to keep up, by playing perhaps just a few notes, and always being there for the final chord. Bit by bit the number of notes achieved increases, until you realise that you are dissatisfied with yourself if you can't play them all.

"I think that this is the first time I haven't felt nervous about playing in public. Any pressure is put on by ones-self. There is very little criticism on an individual basis, only kindness and encouragement, the worst one can achieve being a mildly reproving look from the conductor."

By focussing on the music and how it can be improved, with some useful tips as to how we might do this, most groups do manage to make a better sound than they may have thought possible when first confronted with say, a Mahler symphony or that dreaded Shostakovich overture. Stephanie Cant recalls that when she came on the scene in 1999, the orchestra played *mezzo forte* at all times, but after a term concentrating on dynamics, the group seems to "take in dynamics with the sight-reading". Even in a new group, dynamic sensitivity is "caught" under the influence of those who have already been alerted to it. This is particularly the case when playing with the Baroque group for example, where sensitivity and accuracy, especially of intonation, are valuable attributes to learn.

Yet despite this apparent lack of criticism, we realise that we are being given the space to grow and flower, and whether we are a "returner", a beginner, or a member of the "let's try a new instrument" brigade, progress is almost always made - even on the trumpet!

Stephen Pettitt wrote that "the NTO has grown in numbers, in confidence and in quality". So, also, I believe, has Cobwebs.

For a leader then, there is a considerable challenge, to bring about this growth without apparent criticism, (or by keeping it constructive), and to carry off the "planned spontaneity" which enables changes to be made to the prepared programme to cope with absences, new arrivals, strange instruments, bad weather, etc. etc. As Stephanie pointed out, and as all teachers will know, the most apparently spontaneous session will in fact be the one that is the most meticulously planned beforehand.

From the Librarian's point of view, it is sometimes frustrating to have brought several sets of music in the pads, only to find a completely different set being used "on the night!" – until one realises that the change was to accommodate the particular group of musicians who have turned up that day. As Andy jokingly said one evening, "We have a perfect group here for a classical symphony, what a pity we're not going to play one!" (although he undoubtedly found something equally appropriate).

Michael McKeon in Newsletter no.12 wrote:

"Amateurs do not pretend complete control, so their rehearsals are sprinkled with the squeaks, sighs and groans of music escaping, a reminder that it is a wayward thing with origins and destinations of its own. But they add glee to the work, and there is a harmony of purpose."

It is as well to remember that the word amateur does not really mean "second rate" though often used in that way. It means someone who loves what they are doing. The "glee" is also an important ingredient.

Andy wrote a thoughtful piece about Quality in an early newsletter.

"Quality" is a term that can be quite contentious as it is often assumed to be the same as "high quality" and used as a yardstick against which to measure achievement. This is often inappropriate as no reasonable person would expect a performance by primary school children to be of the same standard as one by adults or an amateur orchestra to be comparable to a professional one."

Whilst we do always strive for the best possible performance out of respect for the music, the almost false perfection created today by professional sound recordists is unattainable by amateurs and can be daunting and dispiriting to try and reproduce. And despite their technical brilliance, there can sometimes be an element of "churning it out" in the performances of busy professional orchestras.

One also wonders whether, in former days, Vivaldi's young women of the Pietà, or Bach's choristers, were always on top form. Later orchestras in the 19th century are said to have pronounced certain works "unplayable" which are now a regular part of the repertoire, so performing skills seem to have varied considerably over the years. Cobwebs is perhaps part of this continuum. Andy believes fervently that the future of music must be in the heart of communities and in actual live music-making. This is where the true excitement and understanding of what it is all about comes, however much it can be sampled in the concert hall, via CD, radio or i-player.

It has been mentioned elsewhere in the text how music-making has an important role in helping people through personal difficulties that they may encounter in their daily lives. Stephanie Cant spoke beautifully and movingly about this dimension of our activity at the first Big Play in Middlesbrough:

"Although it is rare to find this explicitly noted, music of some kind is part of everyone's life in every culture and music forms various functions in both the formal fabric of society and in the lives of individuals, sometimes as listeners, sometimes as participants, and it can certainly be what sustains someone in the face of difficulties in life. Beethoven knew this, and there are accounts of how he went and spent some hours in the chamber of a woman who had lost a child, improvising on the piano for her, and the harmonies reviving her spirits. I think we all know how Beethoven's music can do that sort of thing.

The power of listening is sustaining of course, but the act of participation in music-making goes beyond that, which is why, when I moved up from Sussex and came to live in the North East 13 years ago, I realised how important an organisation like The Cobweb Orchestra might be. It was very small then, but it has thrived because it allows anyone who wants to, to take that step from the joy of listening to the greater joy of participating.

But the Cobweb network is something else too, formed by the power of music, but also a source of much communal life. The 'association' of playing has effectively formed a huge family. As wider society becomes more fragmented because of the mobility of labour, people can be severed from the previous systems of communal support. The Cobweb Orchestra network provides a lot of support informally, amongst ourselves and without being self-conscious about it most of the time. There are always people to take that hundredweight of rhubarb off your hands; and always someone who knows where to go to get a satisfactory wedge cushion for your back. And there is always someone to talk to in time of need.

The Cobweb community also finds time to be pro-active in wider society, which is one of the reasons why the Big Play of 'All Beethoven's Symphonies in a day' shared the takings from the event with CLIC Sargent Children's Cancer Care. Why, you may ask, was it not all given to CLIC Sargent? The answer was that the Cobweb Orchestra does need money to keep going, giving everyone the opportunity to keep playing all that marvellous music accumulated over the centuries, not to mention the new music they inspire people to write.

The Cobweb Orchestra itself therefore, is worthy of support, just on the grounds of its core mission, which is to play orchestral music.

Long Live Music!
Long Live Cobwebs!

Epilogue

As this book was in its final stages of completion we were saddened to hear of the death of Helen Pyburn on May 24th 2013. Helen contributed enormously to the life of the orchestra. She was a Cobweb in the true sense of the word, as a player, an enthusiastic member of the Composers' and Arrangers' group, and a composer of numerous works inspired by events in her life, all imbued with her vivacity and humour. Perhaps the climax of her composing career came with the Horn Concerto she wrote for Sue Baker which was performed in Gateshead Old Town Hall as part of the BBC Music Nation celebration of 400 Years of English Music for the Cultural Olympiad in 2012. Helen was already very ill by this time but her smile was undiminished and her spirit shone through.

The number of times she has contributed to this book (see Chapter 4 in particular, where she writes about the composition of the Horn concerto) bears testimony to the range of her activity, and the care with which she managed our ever growing archives helped enormously in the researching of material for this book, and it is therefore fitting that it should be dedicated to her memory. Helen's husband Mark has kindly agreed to our including a passage from the tribute to Helen read at her funeral and a verse from a farewell poem written by Helen herself. About fifty Cobweb members attended her funeral in Bywell and played several of her works afterwards in a favourite haunt of hers, the Hearth in Horsley.

Having studied the violin as a child in those early years in Harlow, Helen decided to take it up again and eventually joined the Cobweb Orchestra. Music rapidly became a very important part of Helen's life and she always spoke most passionately about the concerts and activities she was involved in, and the many friends she made there. Trips to Germany, Tuscany and Sedbergh were among the highlights she described. As her illness progressed playing the violin became increasingly difficult, but undeterred and determined to carry on her musical activities she decided to take up the French horn. When this proved too much she even played percussion! Over the last few years Helen has also been composing music having received great encouragement from her fellow musicians, and many of her compositions have been played and recorded by the Cobweb Orchestra.

And as the time grows near
Life flutters like a candle in the wind
Breath sighs, the body grows weary.
But the spirit and essence are strong.
Beauty is not skin deep
Rather it lingers in the inner depths of the soul.
It is hard to say good bye to my loved ones
I already miss you.